Essential
Negotiation

OTHER ECONOMIST BOOKS

Guide to Analysing Companies
Guide to Business Modelling
Guide to Business Planning
Guide to Economic Indicators
Guide to the European Union
Guide to Financial Management
Guide to Financial Markets
Guide to Investment Strategy
Guide to Management Ideas and Gurus
Guide to Organisation Design
Guide to Project Management
Numbers Guide
Style Guide

Book of Obituaries
Brands and Branding
Business Consulting
Business Strategy
Dealing with Financial Risk
Economics
Emerging Markets
The Future of Technology
Headhunters and How to Use Them
Mapping the Markets
Successful Strategy Execution
The City

Essential Economics
Essential Investment
Essentials for Board Directors

For more information on these books:
www.bloomberg.com/economistbooks

The
Economist

Essential
Negotiation

anguide

Second Edition

Gavin Kennedy

Bloomberg Press
New York

THE ECONOMIST IN ASSOCIATION WITH PROFILE BOOKS LTD

This edition published in the United States and Canada by Bloomberg Press
Published in the U.K. by Profile Books Ltd, 2009

The greatest care has been taken in compiling this book. However, no responsibility
can be accepted by the publishers or compilers for the accuracy of the information
presented. Developed from titles previously published as Pocket Negotiator and
Essential Negotiation.

Where opinion is expressed it is that of the author and does not necessarily coincide
with the editorial views of The Economist Newspaper.

Printed in Canada

1 3 5 7 9 10 8 6 4 2

Library of Congress Cataloging-in-Publication Data on file

ISBN 978-1-57660-352-9

Contents

Preface   vi

A brief history, and future, of negotiation   1

A–Z   13

Appendices

1 Negotiation training resources   258
2 Specialised consultancies and trainers   260
3 Recommended reading   262

Preface

This book was conceived as a handy *aide-mémoire* for those engaged regularly in negotiation and who on occasion want to consult a practitioner's guide to the many facets of negotiating practice that they confront across the table from time to time. It is neither a theoretical treatise nor an account of the "war stories" of how the world's "experts" conducted themselves.

It is a practical and, I hope, informative guide to the real world of business negotiating. It is about negotiating as it happens, not how it might appeal to fiction scriptwriters or people who imagine the whole world is "out to get you" with bluff and fraud strategies, Machiavellian duplicity, and complex bluff and double-bluff intrigue. That view of business is best left to imaginative voyeurs. Bluffs as tactical tools tend to be counter-productive.

In the A–Z section several bluff tactics and ploys are identified to arm you for what you might come across from time to time – a ploy identified is a ploy neutralised, because for every ploy ever tried there is always a counter. For ease of use, cross references are identified in SMALL CAPITALS but common abbreviations, such as EU or ACAS, may not have separate entries.

Numerous people influenced my negotiating work over the past 36 years – too many to acknowledge here. My singular and main debt remains to my late friend and partner, John Blair Benson, formerly chairman of our international consultancy, Negotiate, which is now managed by my daughter, Florence, who has opened new markets and new clients since she took over. I am sure she would have got on well with John, for he took to and respected hard-working, professional negotiators. He wasn't sympathetic to the other kind, who usually neglected to practise the use of the conditional ("If you ... then I") and who failed to prepare for their negotiations. ("Preparation", he often said, "is the one task where negotiators may ethically gain an advantage over the other party.")

Negotiators who follow John's advice perform better than those who don't.

Gavin Kennedy
Edinburgh

A brief history, and future, of negotiation

Negotiation as a social transaction between humans has a long history. It developed slowly from fairly primitive bargaining between pairs of people as human societies evolved from small hunter-gatherer bands of a few dozen people living in the vast expanse of the earth's continents through to the "revolution" in agriculture and pastoral practices about 8,000–11,000 years ago. Villages and little towns began to appear in the northern Eurasian land mass and spread south-east to India and east to China as farming was imitated and landlords congregated for protection. The history of agriculture for several millennia continued with a mixture of hunter-gathering and small-scale farming in western Europe and the great agricultural empires of Egypt, Babylon, India and China, based on proximity to large rivers and large-scale irrigation schemes.

European trade spread among villages and small towns and their rural hinterlands, creating traders, artisans and marketplaces, which slowly created the commercial economies of Europe. These were followed eventually by the so-called industrial "revolution" in Britain in the 19th century on the back of technologies (some of them known to, but not exploited by, China centuries earlier). The inhabitants of the cities were now counted in tens of thousands and national populations in a few million (tens of millions in China).

With industrialisation, markets matured on scales unknown even in the earliest commercial societies of the Greek and Roman Mediterranean and the long-distance trading routes between Arabia, India and China. Manufacturing and the division of labour on an increasingly global scale brought negotiation to its most refined and complex forms by the 20th century. Contact among neighbouring populations refined negotiating diplomacy at government levels, and in the formulation of state policies towards neighbours and within systems of justice. Wars were ended in outright victory or peace negotiations and future accommodations between victors and vanquished. Treaties of peace, marriage treaties between rulers and complicated succession and inheritance disputes brought negotiation practice into all aspects of civil government.

Traditional negotiation

The essential common structure of negotiation remained as it had always been: two parties meeting as principals or through representatives exchanged their different solutions to the common problem both parties faced, until a common solution acceptable to both sides was reached or the parties broke off in frustration or discord.

The essential common factor of all negotiations was the resolution of the conditional offer: "Give me that which I want, and you shall have this which you want" (Adam Smith, 1776). Each side modified its demands or increased its offers, and, perhaps, introduced new tradables, until a common acceptable solution was reached, or they both failed to agree and sought what they wanted from somebody else. This defines traditional negotiation as: the process by which we search for terms to obtain what we want from someone who wants something from us.

In the A–Z section there are illustrative references to some experiments with alternative reforms or additions to traditional negotiation and comments about their practicality. But overall, I do not expect the existing negotiation process to change much in the foreseeable future. Indeed, this book is largely about the traditional form that negotiation takes in today's world and what it has evolved into over thousands of years, as people explored less bloody and destructive ways, which were common among our predecessors, as they set about redistributing the bounties of nature and the fruits of labour.

Plunder and negotiation

Plunder probably preceded the evolution of negotiation and has always been the singular alternative to it. Violence is endemic among humans and in the animal kingdom generally. As Adam Smith asserted, "Nobody ever saw a dog make a fair and deliberate exchange of one bone for another with another dog." Among animals, dominance in various degrees supported by threatened or actual violence generally decides on who gets what. It was ever thus.

But plunder is not a constructive option, because although violence can redistribute the bounties of nature and the fruits of labour, it cannot create either. Plunder is the original zero-sum option. Negotiation, on the other hand, is the socially evolved non-zero-sum option for both parties. When people value different things differently, by exchanging what they value less for what they value more, they raise the value to them of all the things that they gain, net of what they give up. And because they both gain, both parties are better off.

Our predecessors discovered this truth after a long period of repetitively testing their experiences and passing on what they learned to their descendants. Negotiation as an alternative to plunder took a long time to form as the social norm it became in the modern era.

How important is culture?

Globalisation has brought new variants in the form of local "cultural" attitudes into the mix, although much of what passes for local culture is often based on fragile national stereotypes. It is asserted that the Japanese, Chinese and Arabs prefer to "establish

personal relations first and then slowly move on to business";
Americans are overly fast negotiators – "wham, bam, it's a deal,
Sam"; Italians, Greeks and Spaniards "take their time and are
always late"; Germans and Scandinavians are "very formal";
Dutch and Danish "speak several languages"; Brits are "overly
serious"; and the French are, well, "French".

Of course, these stereotypes are mostly wrong, and the "cultural relativists", who base their detailed "research" into local
customs or attitudes on where negotiators were born, may be
lumping together quite dissimilar characteristics and undermining
the certainties of their assertions. For example, is a Belgian national
of Flemish or Walloon extraction; is a British citizen from Scotland,
or England, or Jamaica; is an American from Louisiana or Brooklyn? This applies across the entire range of national origins, all of
which may affect their mannerisms, and so on. These differences
within national "cultures" may be important, as may whether
they are university educated or of the self-made variety – in either
case they may be no slouch when it comes to getting a "deal".

Moreover, because the research data on which cultural relativists make assertions about how the stereotypes negotiate are
usually based on questionnaires ("Would you cover for your
brother over a road accident?", "Would you tell your boss that you
disagreed with her decision?", and so on) and not on direct observation of how people actually negotiate, they are unreliable guides
for how they negotiate in business.

This is not to say that cultural differences are unimportant.
They can be important, as are the differences within cultures: not
all Dutch negotiators like their country, the Netherlands, to be
called Holland; not many Scottish negotiators like to be told they
come from a country called England; and similarly across the
world. But awareness of good manners – nobody ever got a poorer
deal by being courteous – is good advice for any social or business
interactions with other people.

However, the key factor when negotiating is to be aware of,

and to practise, appropriate negotiating skills. Know when to talk and when to shut up; know when to say "maybe" and when to say "no"; know when to ask a question and what to answer when asked; and above all know when to prepare – before you meet them – and not when engaged across the table with negotiators who look you in the eye and think they have your measure.

This book is about engaging in negotiations with anybody, anywhere and at any time or place; it does not try to substitute vicariously for a good tourist guide to give itself an air of the sophisticated and well-travelled person. The focus is always on practical lessons learned from real-world negotiations.

What about personality?

There are many theoretical distractions offered to would-be nego-tiators, and I would include among them such distractions as trying to introduce "psychological" or "personality" analyses of the vast arrays of people you will meet within a negotiating career. The best that can be said about proponents of these notions, besides admitting to their good intentions, is that they add degrees of complexity to what are already rich behavioural agendas. And that alone creates a formidable problem.

Consider the flurry of enthusiasm for personality and negotia-tion behaviours that originated with the academic work of Jeffrey Rubin and Bert Brown (*The Social Psychology of Bargaining and Negotiation*, Academic Press, 1975). My views on personality, however, are largely negative because I have serious doubts that even if personality did influence negotiating behaviours, you have no hope in practice of analysing, identifying and responding to another person's personality in time for it to make any difference to the outcome, especially if you have not met or negotiated with them before.

It is possible to adapt sound theories for practical purposes but it is less practical to adopt complex interpersonal analyses when eyeball-to-eyeball across a negotiating table during fast-moving interactions. By the time you identify the other negotiator's personality and consider what you need to do, it is too late to apply what you think you now know. Scientific personality testing normally requires nine psychological tests, taking several hours, to assess somebody's personality; and there are 16 possible combinations of the four possible personality types in a two-person negotiation, and many more combinations when more people negotiate in teams.

Everybody has at least one personality; most have a "majority" personality with one or more minority personality clusters that have potential for adopting their lesser personality clusters from time to time. For example, there is how you behave with your work and non-work friends, how you behave in front of your family and how you behave when socialising.

So, learning that the other negotiator responds to argument, say, by becoming rattled and upset, how do you choose to behave? Do you choose to be non-confrontational, when in fact you are comfortable with the tensions of argument, or do you change your behaviour? Possibly, yes, which suggests your behaviour can override your personality. If you can make a choice as to how you behave, this also suggests that how anybody behaves is of prime importance and apparently is not subordinate to their personality. If this is plausibly true, and from observation I believe it to be so, why invest so much in trying to learn how to identify a person's personality mix, which may be subject to mood or circumstances; why not just observe how they behave instead?

Unlike personality, which can be hidden – you never know what people are thinking – it is virtually impossible to hide your behaviours and what cannot be hidden must be visible. People can hide their attitudes and their beliefs, but they cannot easily hide their behaviour while seated opposite you at the negotiating table. What they do – how they react to your questions and to your offers – is there for you to see. In judging their performance during past or current contracts and agreements, you have the data; their past promises count for nothing when set against their actual performance in meeting or not meeting them.

If they are moving slowly, too slowly, and are argumentative on every detail, or resist every attempt you make to tie them down to quality, delivery or returns policies, you might be better considering your options rather than signing something that you may regret. Behaviour is everything and it is a more reliable guide than personality to a negotiator's intentions. If that is how they behave when negotiating, it is possible that you will get a worse runaround from their quibbling and argumentative responses when something goes wrong and if you need to seek remedies from them.

Attempts at reform

There have been many attempts to "improve" negotiating behaviours, varying from the fairly trivial (manipulation using ploys and tricks to "win" by guile, intimidation and being "street smart") to the respectably serious ("change the game" from "traditional" to "principled" negotiation).

The unspoken flaw of the street-smart negotiator is that for every ploy there is an effective counter-ploy. Several are explained in the A–Z section. My advice is to avoid using ploys: when they work, your relationship becomes a hostage to fortune – they might find out they were tricked; when they are spotted, you are embarrassed by their reactions. Either way you lose the respect of your negotiating partners.

Similarly, in their sweeping proposals to change the game in their writings (*Getting to Yes*) and work, Roger Fisher and Bill Ury advocated a change in the way negotiations were conducted. Both are lawyers and are familiar with the adversarial court system of the United States, in which they saw similarities between lawyers refusing to budge an inch in their claims on behalf of their clients, mixed with dire threats of expensive litigation, and negotiators who stick to opening positions and threaten sanctions unless the other party gives in and surrenders.

They call this behaviour "positional bargaining", summed up in the declaration: "It's my deal or nothing!" The problem is that such behaviour has nothing to do with bargaining; it's positional posturing and they set up a straw man to knock down. "It's my deal or nothing!" is not a bargain, it's an ultimatum, whereas negotiation is about exchanging conditional propositions ("If you give me some of what I want, then I shall give you some of what you want").

Among the prescriptions of principled negotiation is the advice to base the agreement on objective criteria. But the sometimes very different solutions that the parties bring to the negotiation already imply their different criterion of choice. Managers want greater productivity; employees want higher wages – what is the common criterion? Sellers want their costs covered plus a profit; buyers want the lowest price they can get to release income to be spent on other things – what is the common criterion? Country A wants to live in a territory because it has occupied it longest; country B wants to move into the territory because it is on its continental shelf – what is the common criterion? A tenant wants a lower rent because it is higher than comparable rents in the neighbourhood; the landlord wants to increase the rent because she needs to invest in a major rewiring – what is the common criterion? Can they find one by negotiation, either by a compromise between their respective aims, or by the introduction of new tradables that in sum would compensate them for getting less than they wanted on the initial issue?

Principled negotiators predominantly find their common criterion through an outside third-party mediator, and in some circumstances mediators can make useful contributions; after all mediation is an honourable profession and they regularly broker successful agreements in difficult circumstances. However, in the real world of negotiating with trillions of negotiations occurring every day throughout the world, handy mediators are rarely available or present. This reduces the applicability of mediation through the "prescriptions" of principled negotiation to a much smaller number of "difficult", even intractable, negotiations than Fisher and Ury claim for its practical applicability.

Moreover, in so far as apparent deadlock promotes the case for using mediation, particularly in multiparty negotiations where there are several stakeholders, it may be more appropriate to look at the apparent deadlock by asking searching questions – and listening to the answers – before trying mediation. As often as deadlock is experienced, it is not always the case that the parties are immovable; it's just as likely that somebody is not listening too well.

If you are not listening, pause, and start asking serious questions about the other party's thinking, the background to their feelings and how they see things; above all listen with interest to what they tell you and not as a prelude to responding with your counter-arguments. It is infinitely better that their answers lead them to revise their outlook and rethink their selective memories than that you tell them where they are wrong. Each question should lead to others, some of which will undo the certainties of their claims and suppositions. If they are not listening, it's the same remedy: ask them questions, not sarcastically or with hostility.

Sliding into intransigence is a sign that the negotiators have settled into the "comfort" of fixed positions or stances before they understand where the other party is coming from. It is just as easy for a party that recognises this to reopen exploration and debate as it is for a third-party mediator to recommend what they should do next.

Proposed armchair reforms, even well-thought-out reforms, will take a long time to spread across the negotiation landscape, much as traditional negotiation took thousands of years to establish a toehold in societies where incessant warfare and the plunder of neighbours was (and sadly in some cases still is) the norm. This suggests that traditional negotiation will continue to dominate the process of getting what we want from others who may or may not coincidentally want something from us on terms we are prepared to accept.

The four-phase approach

Negotiation at root is a process and it is to the process that we look first if we want to improve it. My own research in the 1970s into labour negotiations suggested that there was a common process at work, not immediately obvious perhaps, but after many observations and interviews with negotiators from both management and trade unions, a pattern emerged. It was so obvious that we can understand why it was unnoticed – participants were too involved in the exchanges and their outcome to theorise about the process.

Put at its simplest, negotiations have a beginning and an end; they start with preparation, to various standards. The internet's role in researching in the preparation phase for negotiations has been helpful to those prepared to use it. Receiving an enquiry from a firm of which little is known can soon be remedied by searching for data on the internet. Negotiators have no excuse for entering into discussions with potential clients of which or whom they know nothing.

The other three phases are debate or exploration, and then a mixture of proposing and bargaining exchanges, which terminate either with a deadlock or an agreement.

The four phases are rarely neatly sequential. Sometimes the parties have not consciously prepared; they simply attend a meeting which may not be an intended prelude to a negotiation. Such meetings share with negotiation the commonality of debate, but the participants do not necessarily do anything other than exchange views. Nominally, the meeting may be for the presentation of a review or report, but it may turn into a negotiation without warning. Somebody makes a suggestion about what may be done about an identified problem (a non-specific proposal) and sometimes this rapidly switches to the negotiation of a specific suggestion (a bargain), especially when somebody is trying to shift responsibility to someone else.

During the exchanges of debate and proposals, the negotiating aspects of the meeting become obvious. People present may ask for more time before a decision is made (returning to a preparation session) or they may ask many questions (continuing with debate). If suggestions become specific, the meeting enters into bargaining. If anybody asks a question, summarises what has been said, comments on an issue or makes a general suggestion, they return to the debate phase.

In essence, by being able to identify which phase of a negotiation they are in, the negotiators can select from their possible behaviours those that are appropriate for that phase and avoid those that are inappropriate. They can act constructively by knowing which behaviours work best in which phase and are able to read from the behaviours of the other party how effective they are as negotiators, how much they are in control of their moves and to what extent they are in sight of a possible agreement.

The four-phase approach came from countless hours of participation in negotiations and observation of how negotiators actually work, both those who are highly effective in how they behaved in pursuit of their goals and those who are well below average as negotiators.

Negotiation is ubiquitous in human relations and universal in its application. People who ask which people (meaning national origins) are the "best" negotiators are asking the wrong question. It is clear that those who apply from practical experience, not theory, the real lessons of behavioural interactions, and who gain considerable practice from repetitive negotiation sessions that perfect their skills (not just repeating the same mistakes), make the most consistently good negotiators. The question they should be asking is which behaviour sets work best when negotiating. Understanding the four phases provides the appropriate framework for identifying best practice.

Conclusion

The main point to remember is that proper preparation for negotiation "is the hallmark of an effective negotiator" (John Benson). Time spent preparing is never wasted. Although the internet has taken much of the drudgery out of the professional buyer's sourcing of information skills, it has enhanced, but not replaced, the buyer's negotiating skills by making available at her desk the necessary data to inform her negotiating work across the bargaining table.

The unprepared negotiator has no place to hide when across the table from someone who has prepared and is looking into the eyes of someone who hasn't. Access to the data to enhance your preparation is not restricted by anything other than unprofessional laziness. No amount of bluster, no past reputation and no excuses justify the behaviour, or lack thereof, of the unprepared negotiator.

As Cicero, chief "fixer" in ancient Rome, might have put it:

Ex praeparato, nil desperandum.

In other words, if you prepare well, you'll have nothing to worry about.

A-Z

Add-on

A ploy to improve the terms for a transaction for one of the parties. The add-on is a plausible extra, such as for delivery or fitting or for some necessary component (batteries, wires, plugs and so on), each of which adds to the cost of the main item.

The technique is to quote basic prices only and then add on for ancillaries, or divide your product or service into component parts and set prices for the main components and add-on charges for the rest.

Counter: Ask them what you get for your money before you give a BUYING SIGNAL.

Adjournment

The negotiators' equivalent of a time-out. You agree to terminate the current negotiating session and adjourn for a while: minutes in the corridor, hours in another room, days back at your own site, and so on. You need:

- a break to think about what has been said;
- to reconsider your position or get a new mandate;
- to regroup your team;
- to consult with your advisers or more senior decision-makers;
- to put pressure on them if they are keen for an early decision;
- to rest and recuperate.

Adjournments are risky because while you are absent circumstances can change; for example, your rivals can make irresistible

PROPOSALS or the other party can find a better product or a new client.

Negotiators calling for an adjournment also create EXPECT-ATIONS that they may be unable to fulfil on their return. If you do no more than re-state your pre-adjournment position, you risk creating hostility.

Always make clear why you are adjourning and when you propose to reconvene. If they call for an adjournment, it is best to agree to one. Avoid "valedictory" exhortations and speeches once an adjournment is called. They waste TIME and risk further ARGUMENT.

In some major negotiations, especially when in the public eye, it is usual to agree adjournment protocols. These manage the behaviour of the parties during the adjournment (such as "no public statements" by the adjourned parties, except in the form of jointly agreed statements, no informal one-sided briefings that may mislead public opinion or cause problems for either party's constituency) and limit the freedom of either party to open negotiations with third parties while they are in an agreed adjournment.

Advance

Payment of part (a deposit) or all of the charge for services yet to be performed – but with the RISK of the paid-for service not being performed afterwards.

Avoid advancing payments to people you do not know. If they are short of cash, they could be unreliable. If, plausibly, they need money for materials, buy them yourself and deliver them to your premises, not theirs.

If a reputable business requires an advance payment (get a signed and dated receipt), require a discount on the price at least equivalent to the interest you lose while it has your money. Banks do not lend money for nothing, so why should you?

Agenda

An order of business. It sets out the sequence of the issues to be negotiated; it is a helpful organiser of what otherwise could be a wandering debate.

You can agree on the composition of an agenda but disagree on the order in which the items will be discussed. One solution is to agree to negotiate the items in any order on the basis that "nothing is agreed until everything is agreed".

Extremely hostile relationships between negotiators may preclude detailed agendas that have or imply a specific order for negotiating the issues. But agreement to consider the HEADS OF AGENDA (write them as headings around a circle, not in a column, hence implying no particular order for negotiation) may be a step forward. The less specific the agenda headings ("prices" not "price increases"), the more likely the estranged parties are to agree to discuss them.

Agent

Somebody who represents a PRINCIPAL to third parties. Used in real estate transactions, for the buying and selling of goods and services, and for major contracts in foreign countries.

In some countries specific laws protect agents, not the principal, making it difficult to terminate a non-performing agency – at least cheaply – if circumstances suggest you should do so. Many countries require foreigners to operate exclusively through nationals who act as commercial agents (see GO-BETWEEN), but some specifically prohibit the use of local agents (because of BRIBERY scandals). It is essential to know about local practices to avoid surprise penalties and unplanned jail sentences.

There are four important prerequisites in negotiating an agency contract.

1   Strictly define your agent's authority and the limits to your liability.
2   Strictly define the territory.
3   Reserve the right to terminate the agency if:
    - agreed sales and profit targets are not met;
    - payments are not made on time;
    - the agent is taken over by another party;
    - the agent is discovered to be in BREACH OF FIDUCIARY TRUST;
    - the agent fails to maintain declared standards of quality.
4   Include a dated TERMINATION clause that enables you to review and reappoint the agent or to reassign the agency to another party, to redefine the extent of the territory, to renegotiate any of the terms of the agency, or to take over direct distribution of your product.

Agents who negotiate for principals face numerous problems, including the PRINCIPAL-AGENT PROBLEM. When negotiating on behalf of other people you are a hostage to their expectations. If you settle too low, they think you are not doing a good enough job; if you hold out for a higher price to sell, or a lower price to buy, they accuse you of jeopardising the deal to grab a bigger fee and threaten to sack you. (Check your agency contract – er, you do have one?). Principals believe they could do a better job than their agent. They never tire of reminding you that your role is that of the monkey and theirs the role of the organ grinder. When the other negotiator is an agent too, their role (monkey or organ grinder?) may not be apparent, except when they make excuses to adjourn and refer everything to their principal (like you do to yours).

Negotiating with representatives of labour unions is tricky because they claim a last line of defence before committing to a deal, known as the "reference back" – that is, consulting their members to avoid responsibility for taking decisions in the hope of squeezing extra CONCESSIONS from you. Members are often more militant than their negotiators and they expect final concessions, if not outright surrender, from the other party. When in militant leadership mode, representatives make extreme commitments to their members and bind themselves to extreme demands, making negotiated movement difficult, without them "losing face".

In agent-to-agent negotiations between, for example, LAWYERS, there are parallel negotiations under way; each lawyer negotiates with his or her principal and with the other lawyers. Considerable room exists for discontinuities in the expectations of the four parties and this slows down progress. The more agents involved (multiparty negotiations across several jurisdictions, say), the more complex are the negotiations and the greater is the need for endurance and stamina as the negotiations extend into the night (the 3am "agreement" is almost mandatory) and beyond. All-nighters are hard work for negotiators with DEADLINES associated with mergers and acquisitions, international diplomacy, European Union treaties, kidnapping and hostage release, trade and tariff rounds, and political crises.

Managing their principal's expectations is a key task for negotiators and one that requires open and honest communications. This is part of the justification of the high fees charged by corporate lawyers.

Agreement

The preferred name for a contract. Agreements are on the angels' side of the TRUST boundary; contracts lie just over it. If agreed obligations are not met, call your agreement a contract.

Record what was agreed during the negotiation, not after you have dispersed. If you cannot agree what was agreed while you are together, it is unlikely that you will do so later. If you cannot agree, carry on negotiating until you can.

Record the agreement in any mutually acceptable form. All agreements should outline the action to be taken by each party to implement them.

Aim high

Always ask for more than you expect to get because you will never get more than you ask for. Chester KARRASS, author of *Give and Take: the complete guide to negotiating strategy and tactics*, showed that it paid negotiators to aim high, no matter what their skills were or who they were up against. He made the "aim high" maxim into his catch phrase. His years of experience as a business buyer for Hughes Aircraft confirmed his findings.

Karrass found that weak negotiators (those with low aspirations) made the largest CONCESSIONS and were the first to offer to COMPROMISE, but strong negotiators (those with high aspirations) made the smallest concessions and were slow to compromise. He concluded that by acting as if you were a strong negotiator by aiming higher than you might otherwise, you would end up settling at a higher figure than was normal for you. People tried it, and when it worked they were delighted.

However, the sting in the tail was that the aim-high strategy produced the desired results only if the parties made a deal. If a high-aim strategy does not produce a deal, negotiators may think it is worth lowering their sights a little.

Alternative

If the negotiated possibilities are inferior to the available alternatives, it is better to abandon an attempt to negotiate the differences (see BATNA).

The more alternatives you have, the stronger is your negotiating position.

Ambiguity

May be intentional or unintentional. Intentional ambiguities arise when there is a need for a face-saving formula to break a DEAD-LOCK: "You interpret it your way and we'll interpret it our way."

Employer–union PROCEDURE agreements state that: "The employers have the right to manage their enterprises and the unions have the right to exercise their functions." These rights overlap, and depending on the circumstances and the economic climate, one side's interpretation could trespass on the other's.

Apples and pears

Proposals may be substitutes but they need not be comparable.

With several proposals it is difficult to make accurate comparisons because the proposals may not be comparable at all. Each proposal varies in a different respect to the other. They are similar in that they are fruit, but one is an apple and one is a pear.

Arbitration

The use of a private tribunal or person to adjudicate a dispute between parties instead of resorting to litigation.

Many countries have a legal basis for the use of arbitrators, sometimes making the decision of an arbitrator legally binding on the parties (for example, labour law in Australia and the United States). Sometimes it is a non-binding voluntary arrangement when it arises out of a conciliation process (such as ACAS, the UK's Advisory, Conciliation and Arbitration Service).

If you are unable to resolve a dispute, refer the issue to a mutually acceptable third party who, for a fee, receives submissions from each side (written or oral), exercises judgment and then pronounces the verdict. Alternatively, you and the disputing party can nominate one person each, and the two nominees then choose a third person to form an arbitration panel.

Negotiators cease to influence the outcome if their dispute goes to arbitration. Their case stands or falls on its merits as judged by the arbitrator. The arbitrator may choose some COMPROMISE between the parties' final PROPOSALS. (See PENDULUM ARBITRATION.)

The International Chamber of Commerce provides an arbitration service for commercial contracts (for details contact: ICC Court of Arbitration, 38 Cours Albert 1er, 75008 Paris; www. iccwbo.org).

Argument

Argument is a destructive form of debate.

Some negotiations never get beyond argument. We can only negotiate PROPOSALS. Destructive argument consists of:

- emotive language;
- point scoring;
- blaming, swearing, cursing;
- attacking the other negotiator's integrity;
- questioning their authority;
- interrupting;
- shouting down;
- mocking;
- generally being obstructive.

Argument prevents proposals being formulated, or if formulated, prevents their being considered constructively.

Art of the deal

"If you have what the other guy wants, you have a deal," said Donald Trump, an American billionaire real-estate developer.

Others, STREETWISE cynics, not real dealmakers like Trump, disagree. They say that the art of the deal is give less than you receive to make ZERO-SUM gains at the other guy's expense.

Aspirations

The world is full of unfulfilled ambitions. Some research shows that high aspirations produce better results than low aspirations; you never get more than you ask for. Other research shows that high aspirations result in a higher incidence of DEADOCK.

Balance the prize of high aspirations against the cost of unfulfilled ambition.

When a party with high aspirations meets a party of low aspirations, the less ambitious party sometimes gives way: ambition becomes self-fulfilling. Alternatively, the overambitious negotiator antagonises the less ambitious. Worms turn; they fight back; sometimes they gain enough courage from their anger to reverse their low aspirations.

You should not necessarily aim low; you usually get less than you aim for.

Balance the prize of a poor reward with the price of easily fulfilled ambition.

Assumptions

In business, and in affairs of the heart, assumptions are inevitable.

- Check out your assumptions before acting upon them.
- Ask questions.

■ Listen to the answers for what they tell you about your assumptions.

Assumptive close

A seller's close ploy. The seller asks a question which assumes that the prospective buyer has decided to purchase. If the buyer answers the questions, he (or she) commits himself to buy.

■ Will you collect or shall we deliver?
■ Is it cash or charge?
■ Do you want them in batches of 50 or 100?

If you are buying, seek additional movement from the seller before you give a BUYING SIGNAL. To block the assumptive close, tell the seller: "I am not in a position to answer these questions until I have decided whether to do business with you. First you must tell me what you propose in respect of the following."

Auction

A system of selling that puts the maximum pressure on the buyers.

■ In a regular auction buyers call out their bids in an ascending order. The last bidder wins.
■ In a DUTCH AUCTION the first bidder wins. The auctioneer calls prices in descending order (but see also common misuses of this term).
■ In a "Vickery sealed-bid auction" the highest bidder wins at the second highest bidder's PRICE.

Online internet auctions, such as eBay (www.eBay.com), are well established, giving a global dimension to the traditional auction and bringing together more buyers and sellers than ever before (millions of transactions a day). Sellers pay a fee; for browsers and bidders it's free.

Some negotiators describe online auctions as the new negotiation frontier. Others disagree, saying in an auction, even on a global scale, the buyers compete, with the sellers essentially playing a passive shop-window role and the internet host acting as a referee and holding the winning bids in ESCROW until the buyers receive the goods.

Authority

Negotiators without authority leave you vulnerable if the higher authority seeks additional CONCESSIONS from you in exchange for an AGREEMENT. Avoid this by:

- asking the negotiators whether they have the full authority to settle. Do not necessarily believe the answer you get;
- holding back something in the PROPOSAL for that final traded MOVEMENT to get an agreement.

When asked if you have authority when you have not, say yes, provided you can adjourn to "consider their proposal". Use the ADJOURNMENT to refer it to the decision-makers. You may claim on your return that the required changes resulted from your own consideration of the total package.

To assess their authority levels, ask the following questions:

- What are your company's procedures for making decisions of this nature?
- Who in your company participates in these decisions?
- How long do decisions of this nature normally take?

Avoidance-avoidance model

The application of an insight from psychology to negotiation.

Briefly, people faced with two unattractive choices try to avoid both. The closer they are to an unattractive choice, the more they try to avoid making it.

For example, a company's choices could be:

- settle on the TRADE UNION's terms;
- stick to its current position and thus risk the costs of a STRIKE.

A company wishing to avoid both choices seeks a COMPRO-MISE: a wage increase smaller than the union's demands, but bigger than its own opening OFFER.

The union's debate STRATEGY aims to:

- increase the company's tendency to avoid a strike;
- reduce the company's tendency to avoid meeting the union's current demand.

The union asserts that the costs of a strike are higher than the company's own estimates, or that the company's competitors are raising their wage costs, thus reducing the RISK of a competitive disadvantage if it meets the additional costs of the union's claim.

The company's debate strategy aims to:

- increase the union's tendency to avoid a DEADLOCK by increasing its PERCEPTIONS of the costs to employees and the likely duration of a strike;
- decrease the union's tendency to avoid accepting the company's recent offer.

Bagatelle

A presentational ploy (as in "a mere bagatelle") to overcome resistance to major changes perceived to be too expensive, onerous or unacceptable to the other party.

The "mere bagatelle" is used by sellers of anything that is comparatively expensive. To protect yourself from the bagatelle, always GROSS up to the full cost (PRICE per slice times the number of slices). To use the bagatelle, break down the total cost of your product into small slices.

For instance, sell paper by the sheet; hospital insurance by the daily charge; cable TV by the cost per hour; telephone calls in three-minute units (call Timbuktu for only $1.52).

Timeshare companies use a brilliant bagatelle: "A week in Acapulco for life, for the cost of a week in Acapulco."

Balloon

When the entire loan, plus the accumulated interest, is paid off in a single "balloon" payment on a specified date, instead of in regular instalments.

Lend on balloon terms if you want a lump sum (the loan plus interest) at some date in the future. You are vulnerable if the borrower does not make provisions to repay by the due date and their assets do not cover the loan plus accumulated interest.

Borrow on balloon terms if you expect a large sum (for example, inheritance, sale of an asset) by the due date. If you fail to make provision for repayment you put at RISK your assets.

Lend on balloon terms by:

- requiring the borrower to pledge another asset against the loan and the accumulated interest;
- insisting on a standard security over the asset;
- only lending what you can wait a long time for;
- regularly inspecting the pledged asset.

Bank

Banks lend money that does not belong to them. If they do not lend, they go bust. If they lend money at a loss to people who cannot pay back what they borrow, they may also go bust.

Negotiating a loan to finance your lifestyle can be disastrous. You will end up broke, as interest payments gobble up your income (if you have any).

Bargaining

Getting something you value highly for something you value less. Bargaining is based on exchanging something for something. It is about obtaining what you want from somebody who wants something from you.

When you buy food in exchange for cash you value the food more than you value the cash, otherwise you would stay hungry. The seller values the cash more than the food, otherwise they would do without the cash. At the moment of the TRADE you each get a bargain.

Bargaining continuum

Illustrates the relationship between the OFFERS of two negotiators.

The first offer we make is not the final offer that we might make.

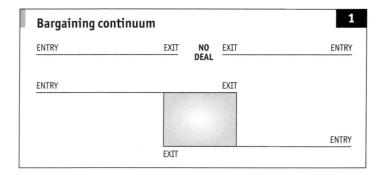

We open with our entry "PRICE". Our exit price is how far we are prepared to move as things stand. The distance between them is our negotiable range.

- The distance between our entry price and theirs is the bargaining continuum.
- If our exit prices overlap, we could settle anywhere in the overlap. This is the settlement area.
- If our exit points do not meet or overlap, we are unlikely to settle.

Bargaining language

Some forms of language help negotiators, others do not. The following language does not help.

- I'll increase my OFFER by ten. How about that?
- Okay, we'll throw in two extra terminals.
- If I improve the payback period, will that do?
- We'll cover the insurance costs, OK?

These are UNCONDITIONAL OFFERS. They do not require anything in exchange.

An unconditional offer is a movement towards giving in. If

they are moving at "no cost to you", keep them moving by asking for more.

Use CONDITIONAL LANGUAGE.

■ If you pay in 21 days, then I'll increase my offer to ten.
■ If you buy the standard software, then I'll include an extra terminal.
■ If you sign the order now, then I'll improve the payback period.
■ If you pay for full security cover, then I'll abate the security charge.

Barter

Exchange of goods and services without using cash; sometimes prevalent in times of war, revolution, hyperinflation and other disasters. Anybody with anything to TRADE can try bartering to get what they want. CHILDREN barter toys because they have no cash. In the "soft" or the "black" economy people trade their labour for food, their surplus food for timber, their surplus household fixtures for whatever they can get for them.

Barter is less efficient than cash, if cash is available, and requires HAGGLING skills.

Remember: It is not what it is worth to you that counts, but what it is worth to the person that wants it.

BATNA

See BEST ALTERNATIVE TO NO AGREEMENT.

Behavioural styles

There are three main behavioural styles of negotiation that are most easily remembered by calling them red, blue or purple:

- Red represents the aggressive, domineering and taking style.
- Blue represents the submissive, timid and giving style.
- Purple is a combination of both – giving (blue) only when you get (red) something in exchange.

Red stylists

- see all negotiations as one-off contests;
- seek to win by INTIMIDATION;
- believe that more for you means less for them (but that is their problem not yours);
- are prone to employing BLUFFS, ploys, DIRTY TRICKS and even COERCION;
- always want something for nothing;
- believe that results are more important than business relationships.

Blue stylists

- generally see negotiations in the longer term;
- seek to succeed by being nice;
- believe that taking less for themselves invests in the relationship (but that is their hope not necessarily yours);
- are naive about manipulative ploys;
- often give something for nothing;
- believe that business relationships are more important than results.

In practice, the clash between red and blue behavioural styles leads to disappointing outcomes for blue stylists. Sometimes the blue stylist is intimidated into submission by an aggressive display by the red stylist; sometimes the red stylist achieves something for nothing by stealth and manipulation.

Blue stylists are often virgin red stylists. Through experience they lose their behavioural blue virginity and become red stylists (initially only to protect themselves from red stylists, but later to exploit new blue stylists).

Red stylists predominate in professional negotiating, particularly in some business sectors (construction, vehicle sales, real estate, bond broking, double-glazing sales), tough labour environments and business liquidations, and in had-tempered divorce, personal injury and libel disputes.

Purple stylists

Purple stylists are assertive in manner and always TRADE something for something. They only trade and never concede. They use conditional language only: "If you give me this ... then I can give you that."

The first part of the CONDITIONAL PROPOSITION is red (that is what I want from you) and the second part is blue (that is what I can give you in return). But together red and blue make purple, and that is a handy way to remember only to make purple conditional propositions.

Best alternative to no agreement

Commonly referred to by its acronym BATNA.

How do the PROPOSALS match our realistic alternative if you cannot come to a deal? The more attractive your BATNA is compared with the proposals you receive, the more POWER you have; the less attractive your BATNA is compared with the deal on offer, the less power you have.

The following will help develop your BATNA:

- List what you would do if you fail to reach an AGREEMENT.
- Convert the most promising options into practical choices.
- Select the single best option: that is your BATNA.

- Compare your BATNA to all proposals.
- If an OFFER is better that your BATNA, consider improving or accepting it.
- If an offer is worse that your BATNA, consider rejecting it.
- If they will not improve their offer, consider exercising your BATNA.

Remember: Your BATNA is the best alternative to no agreement; it is not merely another, better, proposal during the negotiation.

Bid

Puts maximum pressure on a supplier.

Suppliers bid on a ONE-OFFER-ONLY basis, quoting their "best PRICE" for the specified work. Bids are expected to contain a minimum of PADDING, provided buyers enforce a one-offer-only procedure and there is no collusion among the bidders.

Allowing bidders to negotiate their bids induces them to pad their first bid until they see what the competition is quoting.

If further discussion is allowed, this weakens the price-squeeze effects on the seller.

Bid last

A ploy to maximise your minimal chances of doing better in a competitive bid situation.

If asked to bid competitively for business and you eagerly send in your bid, the buyer can use it to encourage others to improve upon it. Hence bid last. Hand your bid over by reliable messenger at the last possible moment.

If the bidding develops into an AUCTION, proceed as follows:

- Tell them to contact you last and ask for details of the lowest bid.

- Blow the best bid out of the water, or withdraw.
- Never bid more than once in a bid auction: bid last or not at all.

Bid/no bid

Bidding costs can be high. These costs are recouped only if the BID is successful.

If you do not bid, you do not win business. If you bid unsuccessfully, you add to your costs. Balancing winning bids with losing bids may not be enough. You must increase your bid win rate.

If, however, you are overloaded with work, the last thing you need is more work. Bid high and hope they say "no thanks".

Winning unprofitable bids is not good for business. Hence:

- What happens if you do not bid?
- What happens if you bid but lose?
- What happens if you bid and win?
- Is there any VULNERABILITY in the contract terms?
- Who are the likely competitors for the contract?
- What can you offer that is as good, different or better than the competition?
- Where are you vulnerable to competitive pressure?
- How can you influence the client to prefer your bid?
- Can you emphasise the relationship between in-service costs and initial PRICE?
- Can you repackage finance and credit?
- Can you highlight cost ADD-ONS of spurious specifications ("gold plating")?
- Can you offer better after-sales service?
- Can you present high-profile quality-assurance systems?

If the answers are positive, deploy resources for the bid. If they are marginal, compare with immediate alternative bids. If they are negative, or insufficiently positive, do not bid.

Blackmail

Influencing another's behaviour by threats to expose something, or to damage something or someone they value. The blackmailer's STRATEGY is to threaten harm unless you comply with their demands.

As a TARGET you can choose to comply with, or resist, the blackmailer's demands. As a blackmailer you can choose to reprieve or punish the target.

There are costs to you in complying:

- paying money;
- changing policy;
- releasing the blackmailer's cronies;
- refraining from doing something you would otherwise prefer to do.

The blackmailer may punish you out of vindictiveness (or to destroy evidence or a witness), or reprieve you if you comply.

If you resist, the costs to you of the blackmailer implementing the THREAT and inflicting the threatening punishment could involve such things as killing a hostage, destroying property, making public something about you, causing havoc, and so on.

You can also benefit from each choice:

- By complying you avoid the blackmailer's threat of punishment (NET of the consequences to your wealth, your policy preferences, respect for law and order, and so on).
- By resisting you avoid the costs of complying and may avoid punishment (if the blackmailer is bluffing or is stymied by your resistance).

The outcome depends on the balance of probabilities of the alternative events occurring. The blackmailer aims to convince you that the threats will be carried out if you do not comply. If you greatly value the threatened object (the victim, the business, that state of peace, your reputation) and believe that the threat is credible, you are persuaded to comply and not resist.

The blackmailer's tactics include enhancing the credibility of the threat (visibly preparing for war or for STRIKES and demonstrating a capacity for punitive actions). Credibility is also enhanced if there is an inevitability about the threat being imposed. For example, a third party inflicts the punishment automatically if the deadline is not met, or there is a record of imposing punishment in similar circumstances.

Tactics available to you are limited if the blackmailer's threat is unexpected (a kidnapping, a hijack) and you have little experience of dealing with the problem. They include the following:

- Reducing the value to the blackmailer of choosing to inflict punishment by encouraging belief in a positive pay-off for a reprieve.
- Convincing the blackmailer that you are ready to comply to delay punishment.
- Stalling while defences are marshalled against the costs of punishment (prepare for war, stockpile for a strike, arrange for alternative supplies, set the police to hunt the kidnapper, make public disclosures of the incident the blackmailer is threatening to disclose, and so on).

Under the stress of maintaining vigilance for "tricks", or merely from reviewing the uncertain pay-offs of the exercise, blackmailers sometimes reduce their demands to encourage compliance. Experience shows that this encourages resistance, because it increases the net benefits to you of non-compliance.

Your willingness to resist depends on the relative pay-offs for compliance (C) and resistance (R). The relative balance between pay-offs (net benefits) decides the appropriate action:

- If $R > C$, you should resist.
- If $C > R$, you should comply.

■ If the RISK of punishment is minimal, you should aim for a reprieve.

The blackmailer has a better chance of succeeding if the cost of compliance to you is not unreasonable and the compliance demand is realistic. Unrealistic compliance demands raise the net benefit of resistance.

Blame cycle

Negotiators get bogged down in blame cycles, because identifying the guilty is easier than addressing the problem. Each side raises issues of less and less relevance to the immediate problem. The result is a destructive ARGUMENT.

Blame cycles are easy to slide into, difficult to stop and destructive of a relationship. There are three things to tell anybody with a complaint:

■ I am going to apologise on behalf of my people for the stress we have caused you.
■ I am going to listen to what you have to say.
■ With your help, I am going to put it right.

The complainer usually cools down and becomes conciliatory.

Blocking offer

A disreputable ploy. A negotiator appears on the scene offering much better terms than those on offer. You stop a negotiation with the first buyer and switch to the new one. Once the old negotiation is dead, the new negotiator becomes difficult. There are "problems", unforeseen "difficulties" and newly significant "small print" in the PROPOSAL. You can either settle on the now much reduced "better" terms or drop out of the negotiation.

If you try to settle and find the new negotiator drops out, you will know it was only a blocking offer. He never intended to do a deal on any terms.

Counter: As a condition for dropping the first negotiation, require the new negotiator to purchase an OPTION for a sum at least equivalent to the margin between his bid and the one you had from the first negotiator.

- If he settles on the agreed terms, his money is set against the PRICE; if he does not, you keep his money.
- Prevarication suggests he is making a blocking offer.
- Go over his offer very carefully and watch out for LIFEBOAT CLAUSES.
- If there is anything in the offer giving him discretion, insist on its removal or amendment.

Bluff

Much loved by scriptwriters with a passing acquaintance with the works of Machiavelli. It is almost always counter-productive. Bluffing is exhilarating from the security of your armchair, but it is cold sweat in the real world.

Avoiding bluffing does not mean you disclose your vulnerabilities. A called bluff kills credibility. Your prospects are dead from then on.

Bobbin' and weavin'

A ploy to dodge a powerful assault on your weak flanks.

All positions have weaknesses. Other negotiators search for them. Damage avoidance is called for:

- **Parry the attack.** I could take up that point right now, but I prefer to do so when we have all the facts on the table.

■ **Acknowledge the problems, but deny their importance.**
Yes, you are right, we did miss that delivery, but against the
entirety of our dealings, a missed delivery is hardly the
decisive criterion of our competence.

■ **Refer to TIME constraints.** I wish we had time to go into all
the details and the special circumstances of the case, but if
we did we would be here for hours.

■ **Refer to NEED TO KNOW status.** To answer that point
properly, I would need to disclose to you highly confidential
details, so please do not pursue those matters further without
the highest clearance from the boss.

Bogey

You convince the seller that you love her product, but your strictly
limited budget precludes purchase unless she comes down in
PRICE. If she believes your bogey you will get a lower price.

Bogeys test the credibility of sellers' prices. Chester KARRASS
claims that the original quoted price can be trimmed away. But
successful bogeys teach sellers to pad their prices in anticipation
of a buyer's bogey, and, because buyers suspect price padding,
they use the bogey to protect themselves from price padding.
What goes around comes around. (See MOTHER HUBBARD.)

Boulwarism

A version of ONE-OFFER-ONLY applied to labour contracts. Named
after Lemuel Boulware, then vice-president of General Electric in
the United States, who introduced a negotiating stance that left no
room for traditional methods of negotiation.

Boulwarism requires:

■ a survey of employee opinion, ASPIRATIONS and attitudes;

- consideration of what the company wants to do in terms of wages and other conditions of employment;
- presentation of a total final package to the employees which is non-negotiable.

Boulwarism is a major BOGEY in TRADE UNION mythology. Because it denies a formal BARGAINING role to the union, it produces considerable hostility, especially when introduced suddenly.

Boulwarism is likely to succeed where:

- the union leadership is discredited;
- the employees are recovering from a prolonged STRIKE;
- the MARKET has visibly turned against their products;
- survival as a company is at the forefront of a majority of the employees' concerns;
- management intelligence has correctly estimated where the shop floor is willing to settle.

Boulwarism is not recommended for the faint of heart or managements that have not done their homework.

Breach of fiduciary trust

Partners, contracted parties, suppliers, employees or others in a relationship with you or your organisation are bound by obligations of fiduciary trust to those they work for and with. This means that a party has a right to expect that their fiduciary trust in that person is at all times protected by the conduct of the person they rely upon to be trustworthy and that they will not act in a manner detrimental to a party's interests. For instance, they will pass to the party all monies collected on their behalf; they will not undertake work for a commercial competitor or disclose confidential information to them; they will abide by confidential pricing decisions; they will not deliberately discount the party's products without prior permission of the party; and so on.

A breach of fiduciary trust can be grounds for immediate TER-MINATION of a contractual business relationship, overriding whatever termination conditions are in the contract, which may include a notice period, being given the opportunity to remedy the breach, or arbitration. But the breach must be so serious that it cannot be remedied by subsequent actions of the person in breach. For example, trust can never be restored by an embezzler returning stolen money, nor will an apology suffice for having disclosed highly confidential information to a competitor.

Bribery

Bribery is a crime. It is immoral. It is unethical. It is unfair. It is practised.

Bribery is corruption. It taints all who touch it. But in many parts of the world it is the way they do business. To cynics the boundary between bribery and paying for a service, or permission to do something, is blurred. You know you have crossed the boundary when you are caught.

Do not assume that everybody is on the take; any country's prisons are worse than their hotels. (If you can't do the time, don't commit the crime.)

Greedy people get sticky fingers. GO-BETWEENs will bribe others out of what they get from you. Occasionally, an important greedy person gets between you and your deal. It costs you a small fortune to get past him. Either pay up and shut up, or shop him and run.

Brinkmanship

A high-RISK enforcement ploy. Foster Dulles, American secretary of state during the 1950s, exemplified diplomacy by brinkmanship. Here is a taste of his philosophy:

You have to take chances for peace. Just as you must take chances in war. Some say we were brought to the verge of war. Of course we were brought to the verge of war. The ability to get to the verge without getting into war is the necessary art.

Brooklyn optician

A version of the ADD ON ploy. The seller adds on costs until the buyer flinches. Supposedly worked to effect by a legendary optician in Brooklyn, New York.

The lenses are $90 … each … the frame is $40 … for the basic shape, like your grandmother wore, and $89 for a designer pair … plus $30 for fitting ….in the shop, and $50 for a home visit … within 4 blocks, otherwise it's $5 a block extra … You can have them in 5 days for $10 … a day. Regular brushed steel is $20 … and it's $45 if you want gold … leaf … 18 carat gold is $80 … a frame … plus state taxes …

Each pause gives the buyer an opportunity to call a halt, which if not taken, tells the seller to keep piling on the add-ons.

You can apply the ploy if you know your variables:

- My normal charge is $350 … weekends extra.
- That will be $90 … plus $30 for delivery … tomorrow … $45 today.
- The documentation charge is $120 … per head.

Counter: Flinch at the first pause.

Buying signal

See one, stop your pitch. Send one, and the pitch stops.

Why? Because buying signals show a willingness to settle on the terms of the current OFFER, so why keep pitching?

Examples of buying signals include the following:

- Assumptive ownership – "I'll make room for this in my study".
- Issuing instructions for delivery.
- Disappointment at lead times for delivery.
- Concentrated attention to buying details.
- Asking QUESTIONS that relate the product or service directly to usage.
- Looking intently at the product. Get them to handle it, fly, sail, drive in it, touch, hear, smell it (the SIZZLE) and keep it in their sight (every glance at it is another buying signal).

Capitulation

The ultimate CONCESSION.

Car-buying psychology

Professional car dealers have at least one advantage over you: they practise their technique several times a day, whereas you try it perhaps once every few years. When buying a volume car, the seller tries to convince you that you can afford it; when buying a prestige car (Rolls-Royce, Mercedes, Audi), you try to persuade the seller that you can afford it. Either way, the seller has got you.

Cash

Instant, perfect liquidity. Also easy to lose through theft, accident and impulse. Insist on cash:

- Sooner rather than later.
- When dealing with unreliable, untrustworthy, or otherwise suspect people.
- When your banker has closed your account.
- When your creditors have charge of your assets.
- When you are unlikely to spend it.
- When the transaction is dodgy.
- When it is a no come-backs deal.

    Refrain from accepting cash:

- When you are paid in dark alleys.

- When you can wait for your money.
- When you have a long journey to make.
- When you are an impulsive spender.

Pay cash:

- When you do not need a written record.
- When it helps reduce the PRICE.
- When you have too much cash on your person.
- When it gets you additional CONCESSIONS.

Do not pay cash:

- When you need a written record.
- When you suspect the money is forged.
- When you might need to cancel the cheque before it is presented.
- When you are not sure who you are a paying it to.
- When there is a delay between payment and delivery of service.

Cash before performance

Used to ensure payments (see HOOKER'S PRINCIPLE). Use cash before performance (CBP):

- When you do not believe in credit.
- When your audiences might demand their money back.
- When the producer might scoot off with the takings.
- When you are into high living.
- When you are only hours ahead of your creditors.
- When your AGENT is ripping you off.

CBP is an opportunity to negotiate a lower fee for a star's performance, depending on how badly they need cash. But take note: performers hire gorillas to handle their CBP.

Cash on delivery

The purchaser pays cash on delivery (COD) of the goods. The cash is collected by the deliverer of the goods (before they are handed over), who deducts expenses and passes on the NET amount to the supplier. Alternatively, the deliverer pays the net amount to the supplier before delivery, and collects the GROSS amount on delivery.

Children

The world's best negotiators.

Children:

- know how to get what they want;
- are utterly ruthless at having their needs met;
- have no sense of responsibility;
- have no sense of shame or feelings of remorse or notion of guilt;
- have no milk of human kindness;
- have no long-term plans.

Parents:

- give in to their children;
- give in to each other;
- are responsible;
- are easily shamed and in constant states of remorse;
- feel guilty (therefore they are guilty);
- are a fount of human kindness (and a bottomless pit for goodies);
- have long-term hopes (pension, career, retirement, peace, "the best is yet to come").

Result: children win hands down.

Children open negotiations on the balance between cabbage

and ice cream with a firm refusal to eat any cabbage at all. You inevitably start off by threatening "no cabbage, no ice cream". Your futile offers move through "some cabbage, then ice cream", to "just look at the cabbage for a second, and you can have the ice cream". Finally, you give in and pass the ice cream.

The children's strengths are their determination to meet high ASPIRATIONS, to use emotional BLACKMAIL and to live for their immediate gratification.

But parents have the last laugh because children grow up and acquire a taste for things that can only be got by negotiation. What is courtship but an early attempt at negotiation? In short, they become conditional like the rest of us. We win.

Circumstances

"Broken noses alter faces, circumstances alter cases" is the negotiator's litany when faced with an ambiguous case. The law tries to be tidy. Human relationships create new cases in new circumstances for which the drafters of the rules never planned.

Negotiators establish that the circumstances are unique and that the ordinary rules do not apply. Whether you agree depends on their plausibility, the genuineness of the different circumstances and the relative inevitability of the precedent being set.

Claiming value

When one or both parties in a negotiation claim the largest slice of the fixed pie. Negotiators go head-to-head, determined to gain at the other party's expense. It is a ZERO-SUM competitive contest in which the winner is the one who claims the most and by red intimidation and adversarial behaviour (see BEHAVIOURAL STYLES), bullying and COERCION compels the other party to concede the claim. Examples include dividing a profit stream, or an inheritance, or any common amount unequally when there are no obvious criteria justifying one of the parties receiving more than the other. Sometimes called DISTRIBUTIVE BARGAINING.

It is usually a negative approach to negotiation and certainly unlikely to enhance relationships. Claiming forgoes the opportunity to CREATE VALUE by making both parties better off.

Close

Just before acceptance, it sometimes happens in the BARGAINING phase that the parties hover just short of AGREEMENT and it is necessary to bring them to a decision. This is helped by the use of four common bargaining closes:

Summary close

You summarise what is on the table, including perhaps how far each side has moved to produce the bargain that awaits acceptance, restating why it is best deal available for both sides and emphasising the benefits of agreeing: "Therefore, can we agree to what we have proposed jointly and set about implementing our agreement as it now stands?"

ADJOURNMENT close

To be used if the summary close does not produce a "yes". You say in effect: "We have summarised the benefits to you of accepting the OFFER on the table. What we propose is that we adjourn while each party consults its advisers and reconvene [at 2pm, or on Tuesday, or whenever] to indicate acceptance or otherwise."

Always specify a time or date for reconvening after an adjournment. Do not leave it vague or up to them.

Traded movement close

In practice, perhaps the most common negotiation close. Note that it is an EXCHANGE of movement and not a one-sided CONCESSION.

By the time of the bargaining phase, when the parties are making specific but conditional offers to conclude a deal, several issues will have been raised in the negotiation and set aside for one reason or another. These may include major issues as well as minor elaborations currently sacrificed to make progress. It may be possible to offer movement on one or more of these issues in order to achieve agreement. Note that:

- Smaller traded movements are preferred to larger traded movements.
- The traded movements can be on an existing issue or on a new issue not previously discussed.
- Traded movements on new issues of principle should be small not large.
- Making offers of large traded movements can prolong rather than terminate the negotiation.
- A traded movement is a small step to secure agreement, not a large step to raise the other party's ambitions.

The accepted bargain

The accepted bargain closes the negotiation. It remains for the parties to record the agreement in an acceptable form.

Coalition

Negotiations often involve coalitions. First you negotiate within your coalition. Their particular INTERESTS may not correspond completely with yours.

Here are some basic rules:

- If you cannot convince your partners of the stance you intend to take, review your chances of convincing others.
- Take a COMMAND DECISION (whether to delay or commence the main negotiation) if your PREPARATION time is taken up with total disagreement between you and your partners.

- Avoid negotiating with more than one STRATEGY or views on tradable CONCESSIONS, and "leaders" with differing views about negotiable ranges. Disarray becomes visible when engaged with the other party.

Disarray in another coalition is usually a result of a dispute about their negotiation OBJECTIVES, one lot preferring an accommodation with a view (the moderates), the other demanding a tougher line (the militants).

Take advantage of these divisions to achieve your objectives by helping the moderate position to prevail, not by crushing the entire coalition:

- Support the ideas, not the personalities, of the moderates closest to your position.
- If the moderates are the majority of the coalition, propose accommodating moves to isolate the militants.
- If the moderates are in the minority, indicate that the pay-off for being a militant is less than the pay-off for being a moderate.

How not to take advantage:

- By pointedly referring to the moderates.
- By mocking their coalition's disarray.
- By personalising their differences.
- By toughening your demands to the extent that you reunite the coalition.
- By rewarding or encouraging militancy.

Caution: Be aware that the militant–moderate "disarray" may be a TOUGH GUY/NICE GUY ploy.

COD

See CASH ON DELIVERY.

Coercion

Facing a conflict of INTERESTS, you can coerce your opponent into capitulation.

Coercion can be a two-way process: each side attempts to coerce the other with threats or with violent or expensive actions. You risk having to implement your threats and suffer the costs of the consequences. Law courts, STRIKES and wars are expensive.

Remember:

- Negotiation is rational if there are high risks of damaging hostilities.
- Coercion is appropriate if there are serious risks of conceding "too much".

Coercion is a COMMITMENT PLOY to do something unpleasant unless your opponents comply. If they comply you win, they "lose" (the Cuban missile crisis). They can also counter-commit, forcing you to do what you threatened. Fear of the high costs of failure may drive you both into negotiating stances.

To back off from coercion:

- Reduce the imminence of your threats.
- Extend to vague deadlines.
- Minimise outright provocation.

Peace can still fall apart with one miscalculated move.

Collateral

Almost anything that the lender will accept as cover for the RISK of lending you money is collateral. For example, the lender holds one part and you keep the other, as with high-value notes, or bearer bonds.

Borrowers arrange a loan against your collateral of greater value than the loan. If you default on the loan, the lender makes a profit by selling the collateral.

To act as collateral the item must be of sufficient value:

■ to encourage repayment of the loan;
■ to cover the lender's costs if you don't.

Your risk in accepting items as collateral includes the possibility that the borrower does not own them.

Collective bargaining

Jointly determined rules for the use of labour in employment. Unions negotiate the rules either directly with an employer or with an AGENT of the employer and cover:

■ remuneration;
■ hours of work;
■ types of work;
■ performance standards;
■ holidays;
■ other entitlements;
■ flexibility;
■ restrictions;
■ lay-offs;
■ standards;
■ work rates;
■ overtime;
■ retirement provisions;
■ promotion;
■ responsibilities and obligations of the bargaining agents;
■ relationships between the bargaining agents;
■ definitions of reasonable conduct;
■ disciplinary procedures;
■ procedures for resolving disputes.

These are the benefits to management in having collective agreements with bargaining agents representing employees because negotiating individually could produce different rules for each employee. There are costs too. The bargaining agent:

- interferes with managerial independence;
- urges employees to show loyalty to, and accept discipline from, the union;
- can initiate disruption in the company;
- can introduce a division within a company which cuts across, or threatens, a company culture based on excellence, pride, self-respect and mutual goal-seeking.

Should you join a union?

- No, if the relative gains from bargaining for yourself exceed those of hiring somebody else to do it for you.
- Yes, if the agent has the superior detailed expertise (he deals with similar issues every day).
- No, if the union concentrates its effort on modest gains for the collective, rather than larger gains for the individual.

Command decision

When a negotiating team cannot agree on a tactic or style appropriate to the circumstances, or cannot agree on the contents of an OFFER, the most senior negotiator can make a command decision by virtue of rank alone. The decision carries its own authority and the team falls into line.

Command decisions are not necessarily correct decisions, but the wrong decision may be better than no decision and, as the person making it takes full responsibility, reckless use of a commander's privileges carries its own penalties.

Commission

Payment for services rendered, for exceeding sales targets, for introducing clients, and so on (see BRIBERY).

Because the GROSS value of an income stream is always larger than the NET value:

- propose that your commission is a percentage of gross rather than net value;
- offer them commission as a percentage of net rather than gross value.

Gross values keep the negotiator honest. Net value is open to ambiguity and manipulation:

- Net of what?
- Who decides deductibles?

Avoid statements offering you percentages of their "earnings from the contract that directly arise from your efforts":

- "Earnings" after their accountants have had a go will not amount to much.
- "Directly arise" confines you to quibbles about how much you did and how much they had to do after you set it up.

Commitment ploy

Methods to make a THREAT credible. For example, unless they comply with your demand you can bind yourself to an irrevocable course of action that would do immense damage to them irrespective of what damage it does to you. The more certain your commitment (you die too) the more credible your threat, and the more likely they are to comply.

To apply commitment:

- Make known your commitment.

■ Show that you mean what you say.

Dire warnings from them of the consequences of your commitment (plant closures, job losses, a long STRIKE, war, and so on) reinforce the impact of commitment ("this negotiator is irrational, I'd better be more careful").

Undermine their commitment using SALAMI ploys. A specific threat to boycott, strike, launch a thermonuclear war, unless you comply, is vulnerable to minute challenges:

■ They demand a meeting by April 10th, you offer one on April 13th.
■ They demand progress to reform in six months, you schedule talks for eight months (then query the details of the arrangements, such as where you hold the meetings).
■ They demand no more than 10% penetration of their markets by your EXPORTS, you send 10.43%.

Salami counters undermine commitment, because the threat is disproportionate to the challenge. By carefully extending the challenge in size and number you widen the credibility gap between their commitment and their behaviour.

Communication

Messages are misunderstood, misinterpreted and mislaid:

■ The message sent need not be the one that is received.
■ They may entirely miss the significance of your message.
■ They need not believe what you are saying.
■ They could doubt the provenance of the message.
■ Your message does not make sense to them.

THREATS, promises and commitments have little effect if they cannot be communicated.

We communicate by what we say, how we say it and our body

language. Body language accounts for a greater proportion of the message received that the other two together. If our gestures say something different from our speech, and this is perceived by the receiver, we have a credibility problem.

A written communication that can be re-read many times:

- has the benefit of permanence;
- has the drawback of inflexibility;
- does not score highly on subtlety and nuance.

This is why others react negatively to what they perceive to be your written insults, callousness, abruptness and threats, particularly in the difficult phase of the negotiation where the parties are debating the issues closely.

Use the telephone to bolster your firmness. It is easier to say no on the telephone than to say it face to face. Use e-mail to make enquiries, quote first OFFERS and confirm agreement (it is not so good for negotiating complex PROPOSALS).

Compromise agreement

Embarrassing compromises are best kept confidential.

Contentious negotiations can slide into intransigence and "no deal" can become (in cash as well as reputation) an expensive legal dispute, in which the only winners are LAWYERS, the world's most expensive negotiators.

You can negotiate a legally binding compromise agreement instead.

- Each party agrees to a binding statement that they will abide by regarding the conduct of someone, which may read something like:

   Mr Jones was an exemplary employee and we regret his decision to resign to pursue his other interests/spend more time with his family/take early retirement. In the absence of his surprising decision, we would have been delighted to continue employing him indefinitely.

Fact: Jones was a troublemaker who caused many excellent employees to resign, was caught thieving, has a major drinking problem, molests staff, almost burnt the plant down and we'll never let him set foot in the place again. Clearly there was a negotiation of the wording of the compromise agreement, as the management were desperate to get rid of him.

- Each party agrees not to attack the other in public or private. The employer usually agrees to a form of words to use when writing references for Jones and Jones agrees not to seek redress for unfair dismissal in the courts. This can in some cases produce references that are "fables agreed upon" or, in really bad cases, references giving dates of employment only and "resignation" as the reason for leaving, with no elaboration of the details either in private conversation or on the telephone.

- Neither party is allowed to reveal even the existence of the compromise agreement or elaborate on its contents to any third party (otherwise the third party would suspect that something was wrong with Jones, and Jones would have grounds for legal redress).

- Sometimes, to sweeten a compromise agreement, the employer agrees to pay some "compensation" provided it gets rid of Jones with no further expense or comebacks.

- Compromise agreements allow the intransigent parties to save face without setting public precedents or reversing public policies.

- They are a useful means of disposing of a tricky problem without risking public embarrassment in a messy and time-consuming public court case, where winning does not compensate the party in the "right".

Concession

Never concede anything: TRADE.

Concession dilemma

Consider the gap between the current offers of two negotiators. You are constrained by a desire not to concede everything. You are in conflict with the other negotiator as to the extent of your mutual concessions. You aim to do better than CAPITULATION. Questions with uncertain answers include the following:

- How far must you move?
- How far will they move?
- Is their refusal a genuine inability to agree to your present terms or are they testing your resolve?

From the other side's point of view:

- Your last OFFER could have been your final offer but they have no way of knowing what is in your mind.
- Should they respond to your increasing resistance to moving further by moving towards a settlement, or should they continue to press for more movement?
- Is your last offer a prelude to increased resistance or to your capitulation?

Concession rate

Negotiators who move quickly at first and then stop are likely to frustrate other negotiators because early movement creates and non-movement frustrates EXPECTATIONS.

Negotiators who move slowly at first then quickly are likely to harden to the stance of other negotiators because quicker movement signals that a hard line produces results.

Negotiators who sometimes move quickly and sometimes move slowly provoke other negotiators to apply pressure because they do not know how else to get movement.

Negotiators who move slowly do better because their consistency is predictable, and if they only move in response to a TRADE they also signal how to get movement.

Concession signal

Negotiators who have a reputation for hardly moving once they make their PROPOSALS induce other negotiators to attempt to delay their opening until their proposals have been influenced.

Negotiators who move in diminishing steps, starting with relatively large concessions and ending with smaller and smaller ones, signal that an EXIT PRICE is being approached.

Negotiators who move unpredictably, sometimes offering a large concession followed by a small one and sometimes the reverse, induce negotiators to expect large concessions each time and to be disappointed if they are not forthcoming.

Conciliation

An alternative form of dispute resolution (see MEDIATON) that seeks to reconcile the parties in dispute, not to judge between them. Conciliation is useful in fractious cases when the normal relationship between the parties breaks down.

Conditional language

States the negotiator's terms for settling an issue. "Give me some of what I want, and I will give you some of what you want."

Effective negotiators use conditional language when making an OFFER:

- On condition that …
- Provided that …
- If you will do such and such, then I will do so and so.

Conditional language educates the other negotiator in how the issues can be settled.

Conditional proposition

Using the purple (see BEHAVIOURAL STYLES) if-then PROPOSAL format ("If you do this for me … then I'll do that for you"), the condition is what I want, the OFFER is what I will give in EXCHANGE (and only in exchange – there are no exceptions). The condition and the offer are always linked and the other party cannot get one without agreeing with the other.

The conditional proposition is the fundamental expression of the negotiated exchange. You get some of what you want in exchange for them getting some of what they want. How much you get for how much you give is negotiable, but nothing is given away without getting something back in return.

Conflict

A reason for negotiating.

We cannot negotiate a variance of views, beliefs, attitudes, INTERESTS, actions, desires, needs, ASPIRATIONS, intentions, hopes, dispositions, EXPECTATIONS, principles and values, but we can negotiate the practical application of them.

Irreconcilable conflicts are resolved by "live and let live" or the outright triumph of one side. The decision is: peace or war?

Reconcilable conflicts are resolved by PERSUASION, PROBLEM-SOLVING, MEDIATION, ARBITRATION or negotiation. The decision is debate or TRADE?

Conflict of interest and rights

When parties realise that they have differing notions about their relationship, or the terms of doing business together, they have a conflict of INTERESTS. When parties dispute the application of an agreed PROCEDURE, such as in a disciplinary case, they have a conflict of rights.

"Interests" and "rights" are common terminology in COLLECTIVE BARGAINING to distinguish how the conflict is to be resolved, whether within the terms of existing procedures (conflict of rights) including reinterpretation of clauses (through a judicial or quasi-judicial process), or through fresh negotiations to create a new AGREEMENT (conflict of interests).

American terminology distinguishes between a "contractual dispute" (one involving differing PERCEPTIONS of "rights") and a "terminal dispute" (one involving differing perceptions of a future relationship when the parties are out of contract). French terminology distinguishes between *conflits juridiques* and *conflits économiques*.

Constant

What is non-negotiable, whether by convention, custom and practice, lethargy, ignorance, convenience, or precedent. Contrast with TRADABLES.

Identify the constants in your business. What benefits are there in having non-tradable constants? Who determined that they are non-tradable?

Examples of constants could include:

■ scale fees;
■ minimum rental periods;
■ minimum stock levels;
■ minimum order quantities;

- credit terms;
- use of in-house services;
- purchase of own company products;
- compulsory insurance;
- exclusive dealing through specified agents;
- single sourced suppliers.

Consider the advantages gained from changing constants into tradables.

Consulting fee

Why do some consultants make more money than others? Because many consultants do not appreciate why they are being consulted.

Consultants are hired for their expertise, yet most of them sell their TIME instead of their expertise. Time costs less than expertise. A consultant's expertise is valuable only because it saves the time of acquiring it ourselves.

Many experts think in terms of what it legitimately costs them to provide the advice. The formula is: divide annual GROSS salary costs by the number of available working days, add a margin for administrative costs and a margin for profit, and charge for your services at a daily rate.

The alternative method is to charge a percentage of the gross value to the client for the advice.

Contingency deal

If you've reached an impasse with other negotiators, don't fight 'em – bet 'em.

Negotiators reach DEADLOCK over differences of opinion about future events. Parties with different beliefs about the future dig in and refuse to budge. Neither side wishes to give in, and if it stays that way, deadlock means no deal.

■ You believe the business will keep growing; I believe that is a long way short of being certain. My price to buy an uncertain business is much less than your price for a licence to print money. The remedy? Agree a base price for the business and we bet on its future performance. If performance is as mediocre as I believe it will be, I "win" the bet and either pay you nothing extra or only a small additional amount. If performance is fantastic as you believe it will be, you "win" the bet and I pay you a much greater additional amount.

■ I believe a suburban rail line will service the new development and increase the value of the houses and the shopping malls; you believe that the planners will not agree to extend the rail line through an area of outstanding natural beauty. The remedy? Agree on a land price for the development without the rail line and an additional price to be paid if the rail line is built.

■ I believe my textbook will become a major seller to economics students and will run to ten or more editions over the years; you think its sales will not exceed more than 10,000 and not go past a second edition. The remedy? I agree to half the usual ROYALTIES for the first two editions and then double the usual royalty rate for all future editions.

■ You have reservations about my trustworthiness; I protest my good intentions. The remedy? We each place a large sum (set by you) into a mutually acceptable third party' s hands. In the event of my defection, you claim both large sums (less a percentage for the third party's trouble); in the event of my compliance with the deal, I claim both large sums (less the third party's percentage). The amount you set for the bet to be held in ESCROW by the third party measures your belief of the RISK you run of my defection. My acceptance of the bet confirms my repudiation of your belief that you are at risk from my defection.

Contingency deals can turn sometimes quite serious differences of belief or opinion into acceptable negotiable solutions that can cope with unknowable, but in due course empirically verifiable, future events. They address the sensitive issues of TRUST and risk and provide incentives for the parties to remain honest.

Contingency fee

Professionals sometimes work on a "no success, no fee", or contingency, basis. This covers some of the risks of PRINCIPAL–AGENT PROBLEMS. If the LAWYERS win the case, the PRINCIPAL pays the lawyers up to one-third of the award; if the negotiators secure the deal, the principal pays an agreed amount over some minimum target. Detectives and "finders" get paid on recovery of the stolen goods, or the release of the kidnap victim (alive).

Variations include contingency fees plus (beware!) "out-of-pocket expenses", and "fee plus contingency" paid as a bonus for success or "fee minus penalty" for failure. The AGENT might go for a quick deal to earn the contingency but may have done better for the principle if more work had been done to get a better deal. The onus is on the agent to filter out the risky deals (or court cases) to make sure contingency fees are likely. Willingness to undertake deals on contingency is an acid test of the truth of an agent's assurances of success.

Contract law

A highly technical subject monopolised by LAWYERS. The advice offered here is a common-sense summary of the main principles, which inevitably apply differently in each country. (Check with your lawyers in your own INTERESTS, but pay for their time, not their expertise.)

A contract determines the terms under which a business or

personal relationship is conducted. It is enforceable at law (though enforceability varies in different countries).

Generally an OFFER to contract is valid if the parties communicate their intentions to be under contract to one another and if the bargain is specified (that is, there is a consideration). If an offer is unconditionally accepted, there is an enforceable contract (providing the subject of the contract is not illegal). An offer lapses if acceptance is unduly delayed and can be withdrawn on communicating this to the other party before they accept.

An offer to contract is accepted if the acceptance is unconditional, is communicated to the offeror by the named offeree, and does not amend the offered contract.

A contract is valid unless you can prove duress, fraud, illegality, or undue influence.

Contracts have six main elements:

1 The identity and location of the contracting parties.
2 What the parties are contracting to do.
3 What the rewards are for performing the contract.
4 What the penalties are for non-performance.
5 Duration, legal basis, reversion and revision rules.
6 Confirmed signatures of the parties.

Co-operative style

Negotiators are co-operative antagonists.

Your antagonisms arise from your conflicting, or competing, goals; your co-operation arises when DEADLOCK leaves you both worse off than if you compromised.

Copyright

Do not sell it for a mess of pottage.

Copyright in a book, a play, or any creative script lasts for your lifetime plus 75 years. Your estate earns ROYALTIES after death. After a copyright lapses anybody can publish your work without paying royalties.

- Insist on retaining your copyright.
- License the publisher to exploit your work for a royalty for a limited duration of 5–10 years.
- Don't give it authority to assign your licence to third parties.
- Insist that if it fails to meet the terms of the contract or goes into administration, receivership or bankruptcy, the licence unconditionally reverts to you.
- Don't let liquidators or publishers treat your copyright as a forfeited asset.

Corruption

No way to do business, but it can be the only way to get into and around some countries just to look for business or simply to stay out of trouble (see BRIBERY).

If you are "on the take" examine your vulnerabilities: the briber has a row with her lover, he shops you both in revenge; the briber gets caught and confesses about you in exchange for a shorter sentence; you fall out with your lover, she exacts her revenge; you get caught …

Cost breakdown

Worth getting if it identifies the TRADABLES and the PADDING. Volunteering one is not so hot; it gives the other side ideas.

To get a detailed breakdown, show a written policy from your organisation requiring a breakdown before an order is placed.

To resist supplying a breakdown:

- Show a written policy prohibiting your organisation, or yourself, from doing so.

■ Claim that "proprietary information", and so on, is at stake.
■ Refer the buyer to your competitors' prices, and assert that this is the deciding factor, not how you go about your business.

Counter-trade

A complex form of BARTER that can take several forms.

■ **Counter-purchase.** The parties agree to a linked protocol to purchase equivalent amounts of goods from each other using foreign currency.
■ **Buy-back.** The provider buys back the output of a plant it provides to the other country.
■ **Bilateral clearing.** The parties export goods, paid in local currencies, which are credited against an agreed total.
■ **Offset.** The buyer is compensated for a purchase by the seller agreeing to purchase goods to an agreed value from the buyer's country.

Traders without hard currency can exchange goods instead. The financing is done locally for each party under their own arrangements. The practice is common where trade finance is weak or the political risks are high.

The goods offered for counter-trade are unconnected to the goods supplied. When the goods have obvious commercial value ask: Why don't they sell the goods themselves and pay me from the proceeds? If you do not want to counter-trade, say no firmly and repeatedly.

The goods are not always of obvious value. Sellers pad the value of the goods they offer, so challenge whatever PRICE they put on them. It is not the counter-trade's "price" but the selling price (NET of transport, insurance, RISK and marketing) of the goods in your own or a third country that counts.

If they spring a counter-trade deal on you after a money price has been agreed for some goods you plan to sell to them, they may be bluffing to finesse additional discounts from you – it is only a device to lower your money price.

Courtesy

Nobody ever got a worse deal by being courteous.

Creating value

When one or both parties in a negotiation seek to meet their mutual INTERESTS by creating value for both parties from the AGREEMENT they negotiate. It is NON-ZERO SUM instead of ZERO SUM, because the sum of the gains to both parties is a positive gain. An example is negotiating the price for collecting hotel laundry, transporting it to a central location, processing the laundry and returning it to the hotel. The parties may be able to lower the laundry costs by jointly investing in laundry facilities within the hotel to save on collection and transport, thus adding value rather than distributing it. Or employers and employees could add value to a wage rate distributive bargain by negotiating a pay and productivity package.

Creating value reduces the associated costs of DISTRIBUTIVE BARGAINING, such as STRIKES, boycotts, litigation and stressful negotiation.

Credit

Give it, and pay it when due.

Credit control

It is easier to avoid debts than to collect them.

- Know who owes you the money.
- Require them to establish their creditworthiness.
- Set predetermined limits on amounts allowed to remain outstanding.
- State and limit the overdue days allowed.
- State the time allowed to pay.
- Set rates of repayment.
- Seek COLLATERAL for the loan.

If you are running into repayment problems, inform your creditors early, because they TRUST debtors who talk to them in advance marginally more than those who are evasive. An unexplained debt excites suspicions and receives most of the energetic attention of credit controllers.

When renegotiating a rescheduling of a debt your leverage increases with its size, for a large debt is a shared problem but a small debt is yours alone.

Cultural differences

They may count. In a "foreign" country you are the foreigner. It is you that is the odd one out. Everything they do is perfectly natural where they live and work. You with your strange ways must adapt to them, not them to you, assuming you want to do business with them.

Take account of the differences, and accommodate them where possible:

- If the Japanese pace of negotiation is slower than yours, you had better slow down.
- If the American pace is faster, you had better speed up.
- If Arabs are not disciplined by TIME, allow for it when negotiating with them.
- If Russians are suspicious, do not behave suspiciously.
- If the Chinese keep asking the same QUESTIONS and do not

appear to take no for an answer, answer patiently with variations on how to say no.

In short, abide by the advice given to travellers that "when in Rome, do as the Romans do". (But beware: you will meet fast Japanese and slow American negotiators, Arabs who are punctual, Russians who behave suspiciously, and Chinese who only ask the question once.)

Caution is required when dealing with foreign nationals and attributing to them "cultural differences" when in fact they, or you, are making negotiating mistakes and not cultural errors.

It is a negotiating, not cultural, error to:

- respond to the other (Japanese) party's silence with offers of PRICE concessions;
- interfere in an Asian negotiator's team selection;
- accept uncosted commitments to translate your technical documents into Chinese because they asked for a "goodwill" gesture though offering nothing of substance in return;
- assume that American corporations are different from Japanese corporations in that you can approach the former with PROPOSALS without a lengthy process of pre-qualification meetings with their procurement people and exhaustive proof of the quality of your products;
- avoid making an assertive statement rejecting a demand from a Chinese negotiator (the word "no" is in the English language so you may use it);
- listen carefully to speeches from, say, Indian or Chinese negotiators but not to those from negotiators in your home country – always listen carefully;
- fail to question closely and persistently proposals from an Asian negotiator in the belief that you might insult him or act impolitely;
- assume that foreign negotiators are not familiar with CONDITIONAL LANGUAGE and that they negotiate differently from everybody else – they are and they don't.

Note that:

- language is the great divide in all countries but we cannot learn every language. Nodding agreement does not mean we agree with the outcome, only with the statement of the problem. It's best not to assume a "nod" or a "yes" means the deal is done;
- mistranslating words and phrases in another language is poor preparation.

Also note that not all:

- Japanese, Chinese and Arab negotiators are slow paced, poor time-keepers, highly reserved and deeply concerned with personal relationships;
- Americans are "wham, bam, it's a deal, Sam" negotiators;
- Italians are excitable and emotional with no sense of time;
- Germans have no sense of humour;
- Scandinavians are formal, reserved and serious.

In short, cultural stereotypes can be unrepresentative.
And you can:

- include senior female executives in your negotiating teams (or be led by one) when negotiating with Arabs or in Islamic countries.

Deadlines

Can help or hinder, depending on who discloses that they have one.

Deadlines put you under pressure. But this pressure is nothing compared with the pressure you attract if you disclose your deadlines to the other negotiators.

Will they take advantage of your predicament? Yes. It stiffens their resolve not to move towards you; they know that you will soon be leaping towards them. So do not disclose deadlines that the other negotiators have no other means of knowing about.

Deadlines that help you are those that:

- force the other negotiators to decide;
- the other negotiators disclose;
- the other negotiators do not control;
- impose costs on the others;
- give you options;
- you control;
- they know you will stick by.

Deadlines that hinder you are those that:

- are arbitrary;
- are imposed by your own people;
- they know about;
- are imminent;
- remove your discretion;
- cannot be ignored.

Deadlock

We negotiate because we face the deadlock of disagreement.

Unblocking deadlock could be a victory for good sense. It depends on whether and what we TRADE to get an AGREEMENT. Many companies go bust because they negotiate unprofitable agreements, not because they cannot find enough customers.

If the most the buyer offers is less than the least the seller will accept, deadlock is inevitable, unless one or both change their exit PRICE.

Single-issue BARGAINING is more prone to deadlock: you resist conceding when you get nothing back (ZERO SUM). Widen the issues, increase the AGENDA and be creative with the PACKAGING of the tradable variables.

Deadlocked on price?

- Pay in some other way.
- Pay less now, more later.
- Pay more now, less later.
- Pay some in cash, the rest in kind.
- Pay in another currency in another country.
- Split the invoice across different budgets.
  Deadlocked on a single issue?
- Compensate by movement on another issue.
- Link several issues together.
- Set the issue aside while settling the other issues.
  Deadlocked on the value of future trade?
- Apply contingency pricing; if your estimate materialises, your price applies; if theirs materialises, their price applies.
  Deadlocked across the issues?
- Amend the specification (what are marginal changes in performance worth?).
- Alter the TIME structure of events (SALAMI?).
- Change the responsibilities (who delivers? who inspects? who insures? who secures? who warrants? who risks? who owns?).

■ Change the nature of the business (from production to distribution; from homemade to importing; from foreign to local ownership; from ownership to management; from management to ROYALTIES; from royalties to buy-out).

Deadlock ploys play on negotiators' FEAR OF DEADLOCK. If they "fail" to agree, they anticipate pressures from the people behind them. Hence they move rather than lose.

To threaten deadlock:

■ Talk up the difficulties of reaching an agreement.
■ Introduce phoney deadlines.
■ Stage phoney walk-outs.
■ Exhibit phoney temper.
■ Become unavailable.
■ Demonstrate pessimism.
■ Accuse them of not wanting an agreement.
■ Make "final offers".

Counter: Show no fear of deadlock.

Debt collecting

Not for the squeamish, the gullible or the saintly. A bad debt is like theft, except you know the name of the thief.

■ Some people do not pay and never intended to pay.
■ Some people intended to pay but find it convenient not to pay.
■ Some people do not pay because they cannot pay.
■ Some people pay only if you make them pay.

Letters and phone calls are useful to a point, but hard-nosed debtors' imaginations develop plausible story lines:

■ The cheque is in the post.
■ I am in conference with my accountant and will ring you back.

- Check with your bank, our cheque number was ... dated the ... of last month.

Counters

- What leverage do you have? Try to run up debts by using their services to the value of the money they owe you and when they try to collect, reveal the NET balance and call it quits.
- Collecting debts is best done in person. Invariably you can collect something towards payment (do not be snowed with a promise).
- No debt is ever a matter of principle. If you find yourself believing that it is, consider how much you can make while you are tied up with an obsession about principles.
- Remember any payment, including payment in kind, is better than none.

Debt swamp

Swamps are not just messy, they can kill you. There is a sense of inevitability about a debt swamp. The more you struggle the deeper you sink.

In the debt swamp you borrow money for a purchase (a house, a car, a yacht). These items have costs (taxes, repairs, maintenance, and so on) as does the loan (interest and principal). If the costs of the loan total more than your income, you get your feet wet in the swamp.

If you have insufficient income, you can borrow the difference and get more than your feet wet. As the debt swamp rises your insufficient income is squeezed. In desperation you turn to a lender and borrow to keep the swamp down; but borrowing more puts you further into the swamp.

Decision analysis

A negotiator's PREPARATION tool.

To choose a course of action (whether to or not, whether to go in high or low, whether to take what is on offer, and so on), estimate the value of the competing outcomes and their probability of being realised.

Estimate the probabilities on the basis of experience Broadly, choosing an action with a very high value may mean simultaneously reducing the probability of achieving it. Increasing the probability of success by making it more likely to be acceptable means reducing the expected value of the outcome.

Each outcome is given a value V and a probability p of its occurring. $V \times p = EV$ gives it expected value.

Set a minimum expected value to assess the probable outcomes against and calculate the expected values of each option.

For example, if the value of the contract is $200 and your estimate of the probability of being successful is 60%, then the expected value of the outcome is $200 \times 0.6 = $120. But you have negotiating costs too, and the probability of your PROPOSAL being unsuccessful is $1 - 0.6 = 0.4$.

The expected value to you of being unsuccessful is your negotiating cost (say, $20) times the probability of this event occurring: $20 \times 0.4 = $8. Now the expected value of negotiating for the contract is the sum of the expected values of each event: $120 - 8 = $122. If this is higher than your minimum expected value, negotiate for the contract; if it is lower, do not.

The analysis can be extended to cover more complex decisions although the principle is the same.

Delaying ploy

TIME changes the balance of POWER and we may need ploys to avoid a decision.

Take two belligerents considering the future of their war. They should sue for peace when there is a stalemate. But the fortunes of war wax and wane. Negotiations are unlikely while each side has different opinions of their fortunes.

Consider a way where each side recognises that continued conflict is unproductive. Suppose peace negotiations begin. What do the negotiators do if there is an unexpected military reverse for one of the parties? At the very least, the winning side has a strong incentive to slow down the negotiations, because each day's delay strengthens its BARGAINING power.

Delaying ploys include:

- quibbling about details;
- taking longer ADJOURNMENTS;
- seeking further instructions;
- "diplomatic" illness of principal negotiators;
- abiding by important national or religious holidays;
- provoking rows;
- feigning insults;
- changing your delegation;
- raising old issues;
- insisting on full translations;
- requesting venue changes;
- cancelling meetings;
- starting late;
- finishing early.

Similar ploys can be used in STRIKES that swing in favour of one or the other party (more employees join the strike or more return to work). Furthermore, the losing party has an incentive to delay peace negotiations if this gives it the necessary time to reverse the other party's military successes.

Delivery

Charge for it as an ADD-ON; demand it as a discount.

Devalued concessions

Negotiators can become greedy. They decide a given TARGET would satisfy them. The other side, say, eventually offer them the target. It no longer satisfies them. They devalue any concessions agreed to by the other party. They "reason" that if the other party offers the target, then its value is suspect because the other party must have more to offer. PRINCIPALS frustrate negotiators who struggle hard to achieve the amount the principals originally considered ambitious – especially when once it is attained, the principals increase their demands. GREED conquers their needs. What principals "need" depends on who offers or demands it.

Devil's advocate

A PREPARATION tool. A negotiator takes the role of expressing directly contrary positions to the ones prepared by the team. This tests your arguments for soundness and consistency.

Thinking through your proposed responses to the arguments advanced by the devil's advocate tests their credibility and exposes deficiencies in the data or preparation, which allows you TIME to fill in the gaps.

Dicker

American for HAGGLE.

Difficult negotiators

Everybody meets them, some more often than they would like. Many difficult negotiators are outright red BEHAVIOURAL STYLE negotiators, others are just plain ill-mannered and a few feel highly provoked by something they believe you or your organisation has done against them or their INTERESTS.

You came to negotiate and they did not. Their version of the solution is for you to give in and go home quietly. Many of them behave aggressively because they confuse aggression with TOUGH-NESS. If they get what they want because others submit, their aggression works.

Your response? Break the connection between their behaviour and the outcome. Don't reward difficult behaviour by giving in to it. Always act in the belief that there are only two ways the problem you share with them will be resolved:

- by the merits of their case (you could be in the wrong);
- by the principle of trading (using CONDITIONAL PROPOSITIONS).

The other person's difficult behaviour is none of your business; it is not a negotiable issue between you. Negotiators do not mix futile attempts to alter people's behaviour (or introduce social reform in foreign countries) while dealing with the business at hand.

Neither match nor contrast a difficult negotiator's style. Matching merely provokes a contest in who can be the most obnoxious; contrasting is likely to be interpreted as a submissive stance, inviting more abusive pressure (bullies love to bully).

Toughness in negotiating is founded on absolute and patient firmness of purpose, saying, in effect: "You will get absolutely nothing from me unless and until I get something from you." And nobody needs to shout, swear, bully, intimidate or be difficult to get that principle across.

Dirty tricks

They happen. They are sometimes called HARDBALL negotiating.

You will meet them sooner or later as a professional negoti-ator. Sometimes you can foil them, sometimes they catch you cold because the other side has leverage and you do not, and it is too late or too expensive to get out from under.

Here are some examples based on real cases.

- Your supplier sends an e-mail warning you that because of a STRIKE at the steel mill he can supply only large-order customers; others, including you, will have to wait until the strike is over. He says all steel product suppliers are suffering and the large-order customers are paying a premium to GUARANTEE supplies. You ask what the premium is and offer to match it. He says he reluctantly agrees but can't promise anything. Your orders come through priced at the premium. You pay, gratefully.

- You call your supplier to cancel an order for machined parts. He tells you that he has assembled the specially fabricated jigs and tools, and cut, drilled and processed most of the parts for which he must charge you, plus various extras that were put out to subcontractors to meet your original deadlines. You pay, reluctantly.

- A liquidator calls telling you that your engines are in his warehouse awaiting delivery but he cannot release them without immediate payment of his revised prices in advance (certified cheque or cash only) because the original quotes were less than cost and contributed to the financial collapse of the contractor, the directors of which he is suing. You need your engines and pay the revised prices, fuming at the injustice.

- You need development land next to the first phase of a major investment now up and running. A private developer who has quietly secured a five-year option from the owners on the adjacent land offers to sell the land to you at a substantial mark-up over its original development value. The owners claim their hands are tied and the option agreement is legally solid. You pay up reluctantly and downgrade the profitability of the project.

■ A foreign government signs a MEMORANDUM OF UNDERSTANDING (MOU) with a foreign aerospace company to buy its series of fighter jets. Another foreign company quietly invites serving air-force pilots from the foreign country for "hospitality visits" to its airbases in Europe, including flights as co-pilots on live missions in its rival series of jets. Under pressure from its air-force personnel, the foreign country reneges on the MOU and orders large numbers of the rival jets, as well as training contracts and ground support worth billions of dollars. The original signatory to the MOU complains but can do nothing.

■ A landowner sells you a block of land for a $40m development but the documentation leaves a 1-metre strip fronting the only exit routes from the site in the ownership of the seller. Your surveyors do not notice the discrepancy and complete the deal. When the development is well under way, the seller's solicitors inform you that you must pay $5m for permission to enter and exit by crossing the 1-metre strip. You are faced with scrapping the development and its sunk costs so far expended or paying for the "ransom" strip.

Negotiator's casebooks are full of similar examples. They teach the hard-boiled that the main element in the duty of due diligence is diligence, diligently carried out by diligent personnel, and diligently checked by scrupulously diligent checkers of every detail.

It's your call. Check your VULNERABLITIES.

Discount

A deduction from a PRICE.

Discounts are given for all kinds of reasons. Some are common in particular businesses and have a habit of growing into permanent features of an invoicing system because they set precedents. For example, an invoice is discounted to:

- encourage payment in time;
- order large volumes;
- pay in advance;
- pay something on an overdue account;
- maintain loyalty;
- place an order before a set date.

After the event, the client expects the discount to continue. Rival suppliers respond to price discounting by offering discounts too. The result is a PRICE WAR.

Negotiators should always ask for discounts, and should be creative about the reasons they require them. Discounts can be demanded credibly for:

- early payment;
- advance payment;
- payment of a deposit;
- large volume;
- purchase of several items;
- permission to use your name in supplier advertising;
- end of stock purchase;
- first of stock purchase;
- reward for recommending supplier to other customers;
- loyalty to supplier over the years;
- first-time use of supplier;
- placing all your business with supplier;
- placing some of your business on introductory basis;
- seasonal purchases;

- delivery at awkward times;
- rescheduled deliveries;
- instant delivery;
- delayed delivery;
- collecting from supplier ex-works with own transport;
- missed delivery;
- incomplete or mistaken order;
- any inconvenience caused by supplier.

Distributive bargaining

Examples of distributive bargaining include the following:

- A wage rise that increases employees' incomes and employers costs.
- A PRICE negotiation that benefits the buyer and reduces the income of the seller.
- A boundary or territorial negotiation whereby one country's proposals reduce the territory of another.

The algebraic sum of the gains and losses produce ZERO-SUM outcomes (compare INTEGRETATIVE BARGAINING).

If we divide a scarce resource between us, what you gain I lose. However, conflict is not unbounded. Neither of us can get our own way entirely (if we could we would not bother negotiating).

Do not negotiate when you are:

- busy with other tasks;
- sexually aroused;
- emotionally involved;
- exhausted;
- frightened
- in a hurry;
- late for an appointment;

- bored;
- angry;
- under pressure;
- meant to be elsewhere;
- desperate;
- under the influence of drink or drugs;
- euphoric;
- suspicious;
- jet-lagged;
- hungry;
- in need of a visit to the rest room.

Dripping roast

Sweat once, benefit many times. Win an order and bask in the income from the repeat business.

Dripping roasts are sound business, if you can get them. Your small percentage turns over regularly, for no additional effort. Don't knock small dripping roasts: they pay the RENT.

Dutch auction

If you have two or more BIDS for the same item, instead of selling to the highest bidder or buying from the lowest, contact each bidder separately and offer them an opportunity to improve on their rival's last bid. This is mistakenly called a "Dutch auction".

Keen buyers re-bid just above their rivals, and keen sellers cut their PRICES to just below their rival's prices in the hope of winning. Try several rounds of quoting and re-quoting the last bid to the rivals (and why not if the bidders keep on bidding?) until only one bidder survives.

Real Dutch auctions are characterised by the auctioneer calling out a reducing bid price; the first bidder to call out in response to the auctioneer's reducing bid wins. By holding back, the bidder risks somebody else calling out and ending the auction. In the traditional auction, the last bidder to call out in response to the auctioneer's rising bid wins.

Emotion

Used sparingly, emotion can help a negotiator express commitment.

There are emotional traps in:

- sending messages;
- signalling expectations;
- underlining a THREAT or PROMISE;
- establishing a RAPPORT;
- overcoming obstacles;
- reinforcing TRUST;
- altering PERCEPTIONS.

CONFLICT generates emotions and can be an obstacle to progress; it can inhibit judgment of self-interest; it can protract a negotiation and provoke DEADLOCK.

Reduce emotional tension by:

- refraining from exciting INHIBITIONS;
- refraining from mocking their weaknesses or setbacks;
- demonstrating willingness to understand, if not to agree with, their views and INTERESTS;
- refraining from emotional attacks;
- refraining from challenging their motives, integrity and legitimacy.

Faced with an emotional outburst, in either attack or defence, remain calm. Emotion dies down more quickly if it is not fed.

It is difficult to eliminate emotions when you have strong feelings for or against the other negotiator for some reason (family, friendship, love, sympathy, likeability, solidarity, suspicion, distrust, previous DIRTY TRICKS, duplicity, unfulfilled promises, and such like). But deals led by your emotions, positive or negative, are worse deals than those that you remain clearheaded about.

Escalation

A measured pressure ploy, sometimes used unethically. Jumping from peace to all-out war is unusual. First, a little pressure is applied, then some more, and eventually full pressure is imposed. If DEADLOCK is caused by their unreasonable obstinacy, the escalation might work. However, their obstinacy might be caused by your unreasonable demands, as they perceive them. Your escalating pressure only convinces them that you are being unreasonable. You risk a mixture of indignation and MARTYRDOM, which results in stiffening their resistance rather than their surrender.

Escalator schedule

A formula to increase an agreed share in uncertain future income streams.

Publishers normally agree to escalate an author's percentage ROYALTIES as sales reach specified quantities. Similarly, anybody owning rights to a product should negotiate escalator clauses in their licensing agreements.

Tactically, your aim is to increase the percentage royalty or fee and decrease the qualifying amount that triggers the increased royalty (and in reverse if you are acquiring the licence).

If negotiating COMMISSION terms (or performance-related pay), go for an escalator clause: so much for reaching a performance level and extra amounts for exceeding it.

It is better to negotiate this before improving performance, as trying to do so later is vulnerable to the HOOKER'S PRINCIPLE.

Escrow

Money held on deposit by a trusted third party and paid over to a party to a transaction once the party complies verifiably with a contractual obligation (see CONTINGENCY DEAL).

In the United States, escrow accounts are commonly used in property transactions, acquisitions of businesses, valuations of rare artefacts (while checked for forgery), disputed ownership and inheritance cases, and media deals where an artiste's earnings are held in escrow until the contracted world tour is completed (it not being unknown for celebrities to WALK OUT in mid-tour).

Ethics

Do not preach to others about your ethics if you want to influence them. There is not a lot to choose between the ethical and the sanctimonious. You should take account of potential costs from unethical conduct, including the attention of the law, public contempt and damage to your reputation.

Exchange

How decisions are made by negotiation. You exchange things you have for things you want; you exchange your consent for a consideration; you exchange something you value for peace.

Expectations

You have them; they help determine your STRATEGY and your OBJECTIVES. If your expectations are unrealisable, or you come to believe that they are, you adjust them or pursue a hopeless quest (see POWER).

Export credit

World trade must be financed by credit to the buyer as well as credit to the seller waiting for payment.

Your options for ensuring payment include the following:

■ **Cash with order.** If you can get it.

■ **Documentary credit.** Payment on presentation of shipping documents to buyer's bank (insist that the credit is "irrevocable" and "confirmed" so that you can receive payment at your local bank).

■ **Transferable credit.** When you are selling as an AGENT, your supplier wants payment when you order the goods for your buyer, but you do not get paid until the goods are shipped to the buyer. The solution is to arrange a documentary credit from your buyer in the normal way, but get its bank to pay your supplier its PRICE to you on proof of shipping the goods to you (this money is deducted from the documentary credit held in your name). When you ship the goods on to the buyer, you receive the balance of the credit on presentation of your shipping documents.

■ **Back-to-back credit.** The use of the documentary credit in your favour from your buyer as security to establish a credit in your supplier's favour, paid when it ships the goods. Less favourable to you than a transferable credit.

■ **Revolving credit.** For regular routine transactions that permit a cycle of credit to operate. As one transaction is paid on presentation of the appropriate documents, another is opencd.

■ **Acceptance credit.** A bank credits you with an amount that you can draw against and the bank places your bills in the money market. As the buyer's credits to you become due, these are collected by the bank to cover the acceptance allowed to you on the strength of your transaction with the buyer.

You can use your EXPECTATIONS of getting paid by a buyer (the credit system you negotiate) to raise finance. The credit is an asset, albeit a paper one. You can sell the credit for a discounted price, the purchaser collecting the difference as its GROSS profit when the documentary credit is paid. Your obligation to ship the goods remains; indeed, the purchaser of the bill can sue you (recourse) if you do not.

Exports

Without these we would all be poorer (they pay for our imports); yet everywhere otherwise sensible people seek to curb each other's.

Exporting is complicated. Frontiers are jealousy guarded. Legal systems differ throughout the world and disputes between people in separate territories – with the goods, perhaps, in a third territory or in transit between them – add to the normal complexities (and costs). The number of intermediaries involved in shipping goods imposes heavy demands on comprehensive documentation, title to ownership, transfer of ownership and timely payment as agreed between seller and buyer. At a minimum, documentation is required to describe the goods, to value them and to authenticate the declaration. The shipper (by vessel, vehicle or aircraft) has numerous formalities to complete too. These formalities, and their associated costs, incline the prudent seller towards an ex-works PRICE for the goods, leaving the hassle of exporting and importing to the buyer.

Factoring

Invoices are bought by a factoring agency, which collects payment from the buyers and pockets the difference between what it pays for the invoices and what it collects.

The factoring agency eliminates known bad payers, or potential bad payers, and requires a larger margin on some others. Some agencies use the supplier's own notepaper, so buyers are unaware they are dealing with a factor.

The spread between the factoring PRICE and the invoice's face value is negotiable, as is whether the factor has recourse to the seller in the case of a bad debt.

Failure to agree

A formal declaration required in COLLECTIVE BARGAINING procedure agreements when negotiators cannot settle the dispute at their level. Sometimes negotiators fail to agree on the "nod", so that an issue can reach an appropriate level more quickly.

Fair

A sense of fairness influences negotiators (see NASH SOLUTION). If you were asked what you would regard as a fair distribution of a large sum of money between you and a colleague, and you were given no additional information, it is likely that you would prefer an "equal distribution".

Fairness as a settlement option is popular with economists

because their negotiation models do not incorporate BARGAIN-ING skills, POWER perceptions and EXPECTATIONS. By eliminating these, the settlement must end up at the mid-point, because there is no economic reason why it should end up anywhere else.

Fairness, however, is not a principle of nature; it is a construct of the mind.

Fait accompli

A ploy to shift POWER to the doer and raise the stakes if counter-sanctions are applied.

- Armies seize territory and then offer to negotiate.
- A developer knocks down a unique building and then applies for planning permission.
- Managers introduce new work schedules and then agree to negotiations.
- Buyers send a cheque for a lesser amount than the disputed invoice.
- A buyer returns goods outside WARRANTY and refuses to pay.
- A department occupies disputed office space and offers talks.

Counter: Write into your contract firm rules on what cannot be done without invoking heavy penalties.

Fall-back

If you have not got one, then you stand and fight where you are. Best to think about a fall-back stance if the negotiations do not work out as you expected. (See BATNA.)

Fear of deadlock

Common enough in negotiation. Fear inhibits negotiators from standing firm, encourages GOODWILL concessions and opens them to exploitation. DEADLOCK implies "failure" and we do not like to fail. Much better to overcome the fear, and certainly never to disclose it.

Final offer

If you make one, mean it; otherwise do not make one. Final offers are risky and are foolhardy at the beginning of a negotiation. Final offers that become "final offers but one" (or two, or three) are disastrous for credibility. A "final offer" BLUFF, if called, is embarrassing.

To make final offers, pay attention to your language. If no more movement is possible – you are at your exit point and prefer no deal to one on worse terms – convey this. A badly phrased final offer, however, is a provocative ultimatum. Tell them:

- you can go "no further";
- you are at the "end of the road";
- that it is "decision time".

None of these statements mentions final offer, but that is how it will be perceived.

Do not ask: Is that your final offer? The answer you get is not the one you want. They can hardly say no (the answer you want) without compromising their position, hence they are most likely to say yes, blocking off further negotiation.

First offer

Never accept a first offer: negotiate.

The first offer is where they open; it is not where they expect to end up. If it is, they are in such a powerful position that there is no need to negotiate.

If you accept their first offer, what other (better) offers would you accept?

Fixed price

Sellers love fixed prices because they preclude BARGAINING. That is why they write PRICES on large tickets, print price lists, have standard terms for doing business and imply that the price on the tag is fixed for good. And why not? Most people accept fixed prices. Few challenge them, and fewer still persist after the first no.

But the price on the tag, or printed on the list, is their FIRST OFFER. Whether it is their FINAL OFFER remains to be seen.

More often than not, the aversion to negotiating a better price has nothing to do with the buyer's relative POWER. It is part of the business culture you live in. In the UK, 97% of people accept the buyer's first offer; in the United States, it is down as low as 17% in some commodity groups; in Australia, it is around 30%.

In business transactions, however, effective negotiators do not accept the price they are first quoted. They:

- haggle;
- try to open up first offers to discussion;
- see what other offers are lurking in the background. (See DISCOUNT.)

Flexibility

In short supply among average negotiators. Flexibility in approach, not INTERESTS, comes from thorough PREPARATION. The above-average negotiator is armed with options, in terms of both goals and methods of achieving them.

Force majeure

Excusable delay – events that are outside the control of the contracting parties and that prevent a contractual obligation being
met. Revolutions, war, seizure of assets, embargoes, economic
sanctions, geological and climatic disturbances and suchlike can
make fulfilment of a contract impossible, or severely delay completion. Include *force majeure* provisions in your contract (with
wide terms if supplying and narrow terms if receiving).

Force projection

An indirect pressure ploy.

Unions use force projection in contract negotiations. They hold
a mass march, demonstration or assembly easily seen by the managers. A disturbance, a few arrests, TV coverage of a police baton
charge or fiery speeches all contribute to force projection (in this
case, projecting their determination and support).

Buyers' force projection measures include:

- open contact with competition;
- competitors' notepaper visible on desk;
- in-house costings in "make or buy?" reports;
- circular letter calling for tenders.

Sellers' force projection measures include:

- surcharges on small orders;
- lengthy delivery dates;
- publicity about growing market share;
- acquisition of, or merger with, rivals.

All force projection measures aim to influence the negotiators'
EXPECTATIONS.

Forfaiting

Subject to certain conditions, a bank forfaits an invoice for an exporter by paying direct to the exporter an agreed proportion of its face value. The bank then assumes total responsibility for collecting the money from the importer, and usually does not have recourse to the exporter if its customer fails to pay.

The difference between the exporter's income from the bank and the face value of the invoice is justified by the certainty of payment compared with the usual RISKS faced by exporters. The terms of the forfaiting facility are negotiable.

Formula bargaining

An analytical approach to international diplomacy that divides negotiation into three phases:

■ pre-negotiations or "diagnostic" phase;
■ defining the appropriate "formula" phase;
■ the "detail" phase.
  Negotiators are advised to:
■ pay attention to the facts, the history of the problem, and how it has evolved;
■ look for precedents and how referents governing similar situations have developed;
■ know about the specific contexts and PERCEPTIONS of the disputants and how they perceive their INTERESTS.

The negotiators engage in a search for an agreed formula that refers to:

■ an agreed definition of the conflict;
■ cognitive referents that imply a solution;
■ some criterion of justice.

Negotiators must "remember that the problem, not the other party, is the 'enemy' to be overcome".

The detail phase of the negotiations is a hard slog though the itemised applications of the formula. Care is needed to:

- keep the "big picture" in focus while negotiating the details;
- be able to match flexibility with steadfastness in pursuit of clearly defined OBJECTIVES;
- handle the "eyeball-to-eyeball" moments in major international negotiations where there is a knife-edge between success and resort to other options.

Four phases

All negotiations are different. They are also all the same, in that they share a common four-phase process: prepare, debate (or explore), propose and bargain.

1 Prepare. Best done before you negotiate; often not done properly (if at all). Preparation answers the question: what do we want?

By preparing properly you gain command of the detail ("In God we trust, all others must provide data"). You think through what it is you want; you consider your INTERESTS; you anticipate responses, counters and themes that may be exchanged in the debate; you identify the negotiable issues and your priorities, and what may be the interests, issues and priorities of the other party.

2 Debate (explore). You can choose to be constructive or destructive. It's better to use the TIME for finding out what the other party wants and why. Debate answers the question: what do they want?

In negotiation you start with two solutions: yours and the other party's. The object is to find a third solution acceptable to both of you. Time spent arguing delays the exploration of possible solutions that are different from the ones you started with. Constructive debate behaviours include: asking QUESTIONS (and

LISTENING to the answers); SUMMARISING (brief, neutral and true); and SIGNALLING.

3 Propose. Make tentative suggestions that point to a solution, always in CONDITIONAL LANGUAGE ("if you were to consider doing this for me, than I would be prepared to consider doing that for you") but not as an unassertive question ("if I did this for you, would you do that for me?").

4 Bargain. A specific conditional OFFER: "If you do X, then I will do Y." Bargains invite a "yes" response, which CLOSES the negotiation. If the response is "no", the negotiation continues by returning to the debate phase or by attracting a counter-bargain.

The phases do not necessarily follow the same order and they can be repeated in different combinations of sequences. A negotiation can open with a bargain – a specific solution for acceptance or negotiation. If the proposed bargain requires a detailed assessment, the receiving party may return to the preparation phase to examine its implications and compare with other potential solutions. If the receiving party asks a question about the bargain, the negotiation moves to the debate phase. A negotiation may open with a tentative PROPOSAL, which will certainly require debate and may require detailed PREPARATION too.

The phases are different sets of negotiating behaviours. The appropriate behaviours for each phase can be learned and practised to improve negotiating performance.

Friendship

Neither necessary nor sufficient to get an AGREEMENT, but seldom a hindrance.

The personal relations of the negotiators can be warmer than the relations between the constituents they represent. This is not an uncommon experience in difficult (for example, peace treaty) negotiations.

Working on the interpersonal relationship can help, but in some contexts it can hinder. For example, negotiating with officials from a bureaucracy can lead to misunderstandings if your friendly gestures are thought to be enticing them into corrupt or disloyal stances. Certainly, if you are on good personal terms with the other side it is better than being hardly able to speak to them, but remember, the exploitation of the friendship is not all one way (they get to you too).

Frontal assault

A high-RISK ploy to compromise the other negotiator's credibility.

- That is not what your predecessor said to us last time we met.
- Perhaps you should adjourn and consult with your people in more detail before you dig in too deep on this issue.

The other negotiator is irritated by this ploy and may "blow her top". It could sour your relationship for good. Use rarely.

Game theory

Mathematical formulation of conflict dilemmas applied to the BARGAINING problem.

- The identity of the players and their number are fixed and known to everyone (you are not playing against the anonymous "MARKET").
- All players are rational and everybody knows they are rational.
- The pay-offs of each player are known to each player.
- Each player's strategies are known and fixed.
- Bargaining skills are assumed to be equal.

The manipulation of available information for personal advantage between the players is limited, but not excluded, by the assumptions.

Two-person ZERO-SUM games show that players in a pure conflict game assume that the other person is malevolent and therefore disposed to "do his worst" whatever STRATEGY is selected. A player does best by selecting the strategy that assures the "best of the worst outcomes".

Two-person NON-ZERO-SUM games are more complex. The degree of strategic interaction increases dramatically as they explore opportunities for mutual gain. (See NASH SOLUTION and PRISONER'S DILEMMA.)

Gazump

You think you have a contract. The other party considers it to be an intention. Somebody else offers them a better deal. So they drop their deal with you and sign a contract with them. You have been gazumped.

Gazumping can be inconvenient if you are relying on the transaction going through.

Gazumping may be the only option you have if the other party is unable to close the deal within a reasonable period of time, or you need the deal more than you are concerned about the ETHICS of gazumping. Hence you gazump.

To avoid gazumping, negotiate an exclusive OPTION.

Generosity

Not contagious without a high degree of TRUST between the negotiators. Making an UNCONDITIONAL OFFER does not promote reciprocal GOODWILL. The other negotiators perceive you to be in a weaker position, and may revise their initial demands accordingly.

Unless and until you develop a strong relationship with the other negotiator, be like Scrooge rather than St Francis of Assisi.

Get-between

Unlike a GO-BETWEEN hired to do a job, a get-between appears, uninvited, clutching an OPTION from the owners of a business or a land purchase, or whatever, and gets between you and the deal.

This happens only if you have been too casual about covering your obvious VULNERABLITIES in a deal and expect to make easy progress. Other people read the newspapers; keep in touch with business gossip; visit the planning offices and see your intentions; visit the site before anything is built and see its boundaries and where you will need to expand, or where the choke points are in the business you intend to acquire (PATENTS AND LICENCES, lack of registered trademarks, distribution outlets, inspection regimes, suppliers of essential inputs, local labour sources, residences for incoming executives, security requirements, and so on) and take action to have control over them, forcing you to deal with them, perhaps when it is least convenient.

Get-betweens cost you money, perhaps lots of it, just to get them out of the way. They are avoided by proper audits of your vulnerabilities downstream and a willingness to cover them even if it costs you exclusive option money. Don't rely on the "cover" allegedly provided by intimate contacts with the local political bigwigs – they may be behind the get-between's appearance and might be funding it. And watch out for phoney get-betweens. You think they are genuine but their "options" are not. Check their claims. At the very least, demand to see them.

Get it in writing

"My word is my bond," they said in a bygone age, but their notarised written contract is better than their oral bond – it ties them to the promises they made to get the deal.

Remember:

- If you have it in writing you have a prayer.
- If it ain't in writing, you've got thin air.

Getting out from under

Deals go sour. If you are in the pit, stop digging: get out from under.

We hang on in the hope that something will turn up. To give

up is a defeat, a sign of weakness, a confession of failure. Right? Wrong. Digging in when we have clearly made a mistake is for dumbos.

If you can't avoid the occasional lemon, get rid of it when you realise you've got one. After you've got out from under, study why you got into the mess in the first place and try not to make the same mistake twice.

Getting paid

Not everybody gets paid what they are due. Getting paid is sometimes more difficult than doing the work you have not been paid for.

There can be genuine differences of opinions as to:

- how much is owed;
- what the agreed PRICE was;
- who was responsible for the revisions and variations;
- the quality of the completed work.

There can also be wholly unscrupulous reasons for failures to pay.

Well-structured variation procedures identify the obligation to pay and well-thought-out and disciplined invoicing systems help you to collect your money. (See CREDIT CONTROL.)

Give and take

A description of the negotiator's trading behaviour. A caveat:

- "giving" does not cause "getting";
- "taking" does not cause "giving".

Trading requires linked give and take – one goes with the other – and therefore only offer to give if you simultaneously get something back in exchange.

Go-between

Trade name for someone akin to an AGENT, particularly in the Middle East.

A go-between is usually a national of the importing country who acts as the contact person between you and the importer. It is not always clear exactly who the go-between acts for, but several countries insist that foreigners do all their business through a local national. In exchange for handling the transactions between the parties, the go-between receives a COMMISSION paid out of the foreigner's share of the transaction.

As go-betweens often also act for the other party, or at least are candid with them about your limits, they can hardly be described as bona fide agents. Their status is inescapably ambiguous. Casual recruitment of a go-between can prove expensive. Consult your embassy's commercial attaché before embarking on a contract with a go-between.

Goodwill

Earned but not given automatically.

Conceding something, no matter how little, in order to "create goodwill" is futile. The other negotiators stiffen their position when you make UNCONDITIONAL OFFERS. Moreover, the "little" things you give away may acquire considerable leverage potential later in the negotiation – they could even clinch the AGREEMENT if offered at the right time – and throwing them away, in the futile hope of creating goodwill, is extremely costly when the result is that you have nothing left to close the deal.

Greed

Snatching DEADLOCK out of the jaws of compromise by being too greedy.

You do not intend to be greedy, only ambitious. The other negotiator resents your greed and resists. You end up with nothing.

Grievance

Don't just state a grievance, propose a remedy.

Concentrate your attention on your grievance and you are likely to argue. Think about what you want done about your grievance, select a proportionate remedy within the other negotiator's gift (beware of GREED) and you are likely to enjoy the remedy sooner than you will settle an ARGUMENT.

Gross

The gross of anything is larger than the NET.

A percentage of gross income is worth more than a percentage of gross profit, and both are worth more than a percentage of net income or net profit respectively. This is especially true when the other negotiator controls the calculation of the net.

Guanxi

Traditional personal relationships cemented by continuous reciprocal favours in China.

Guanxi (pronounced "gwanshee") reflects limited resource allocation by market prices in China and the need to use the alternative of *guanxi* networks to allocate resources, including official permissions and licences, to get things done by whom, not what, you know. In the absence of PRICE allocation, personal relationships are more valued than MARKET efficiency.

Although officially disapproved of, *guanxi* allegedly permeates Chinese business life. The obverse is that an anonymous rival's quiet but powerful *guanxi* relationships may block your project mysteriously – you have chosen the "wrong" partners who don't have the right, or enough, *guanxi*.

Rising commercialism and growing reliance on markets might explain why *guanxi* may be in decline, particularly among younger, more market-oriented mainland Chinese.

Guarantee

Of great value where the risks of non-compliance are high. Banks demand guarantees to cover their loans; clients want guarantees to cover your performance (see PERFORMANCE BOND); you like guarantees when it's your money at stake.

- Make sure when giving guarantees that you can pay up if things go wrong ("Murphy's Law" is no joke).
- Extravagant guarantees are dangerous.
- Ask for guarantees.
- If they cannot guarantee something, adjust the price downwards.
- If they guarantee something as a matter of course, ask for a PRICE without the guarantee (you are paying for it in an insurance premium anyway).
- If the guarantee needs to be invoked, consider a payment in lieu of litigation to collect it.

Haggle

A noble art. The seller discovers the maximum a buyer will pay, without disclosing the minimum he or she will accept (and vice versa).

Haggling is part theatre. Effective hagglers:

■ give plausible reasons for you to improve your OFFER;
■ rely on sympathy, emotions, their "facts" and your lack of stamina;
■ use mutual convergence between their and your current PRICES to secure an AGREEMENT;
■ use silence effectively while waiting for you to move;
■ enter high or low to create room to move more slowly in smaller steps towards you than you move in larger steps towards them.

Hardball negotiating

Hardballs, like baseballs and cricket balls, hurt. Hardball negotiators are tough and like making "offers you cannot refuse", as when they:

■ hold your "markers" (acknowledgements of your gambling debts);
■ have embarrassing information unknown to your partners or spouse;
■ know you need the deal so badly you are sweating blood to get it;
■ have the bedroom photos of you caught in a "honey trap";

■ hold and threaten someone near and dear to you.

Heads of agenda

A useful device to get stalled talks restarted.

Your differences with the other side could be sharp. You find it impossible to:

■ handle all the differences;
■ decide which issues should be tackled first;
■ choose which issues should be tackled at all;
■ separate out the poisoned relations between the parties.

Try for a heads of agenda that does not contain PROPOSALS and requires no explanation. Agree a set of headings of the issues you want to discuss. These need not be placed in any particular order (write the items in a circle, not as a column). If you can agree on even a restricted list of headings, this could precipitate enough momentum to allow the negotiations to recommence.

Heads of agreement

A device for reaching basic agreement on the broad issues before settling the contractual details, much used in property negotiations. Often used after preliminary meetings to record general agreement on main headings. Can be useful as statement of interest (sometimes called a MEMORANDUM OF UNDERSTANDING).

But caution is required, especially in cross-border negotiations, because different jurisdictions (for example, China) might give higher status to such statements than you intended and may regard specific commitments as binding agreements.

Always start heads of agreement with "Subject to contract", and do not accept verbal assurances of their being "mere formalities to show the authorities you are serious about doing business". "Heads" can imply limited "solutions" to issues by listing them. For example, the heading "annual increase in charges" presupposes that charges are to be increased annually, when you prefer the heading to read "changes in charges by mutual consent". This heading is neutral; charges may be changed (increased or decreased, or remain the same), but always by mutual consent, leaving you both a veto.

Avoid mentioning specific PRICE references and currencies. It is best to write "pricing and currency to be agreed", or something similar, next to all references to quantifiable issues.

Hooker's principle

Services are valued more highly before they are performed than they are afterwards. It is better to be paid before you provide a service.

When, for instance, does a plumber's fee look reasonable? When you are up to your knees in water. Always agree the basis on which you expect to be paid before you do the work. They are more likely to agree to pay your (high) charge while they feel the pressure of their crisis than they are afterwards.

Hospitality

Welcome but dangerous. Hospitality exposes you to CONCESSION by obligation.

Hospitality is part of the furniture of social relationships. To refuse hospitality could be unhelpful to your chances. To partake, especially at an overly generous level (and your host controls the level), could imply obligations that you did not intend, and raise QUESTIONS from your side about your objectivity under a barrage of hospitality.

Hospitality can be used to:

- weaken your resolve;
- undermine your stamina (late nights, heavy drinking);
- entrap you into indiscretion.

It can also be a genuine expression of a desire to do business together. How do you know which it is? Follow some rules:

- Insist on the RECIPROCITY of equivalents – each side is hospitable to the other on the same basis.
- Do not compete on levels of hospitality.
- Do not socialise late every night (they have a supply of sociable people to keep you at it while their negotiators rest).
- Strictly limit your consumption of food, drink and tobacco.
- Schedule your caucus sessions for most evenings so that you can decline an invitation without offence.
- Insist that "both sides bear their own costs".
- Cut out business lunches (they are mostly unproductive and disruptive of the afternoon's schedules).
- Negotiate in working hours only (difficult in some circumstances).

Hostage negotiation

Hostages are taken either for material gain (cash) or for political influence (publicity, revenge, humbling of an enemy, recognition, release of prisoners, change in policies). Terrorist extortion produces a common dilemma: if the demands are conceded, a spate of imitations can be expected; if the demands are not met, the hostages could be harmed.

Governments are less likely to concede demands for political influence than they are demands for material gains.

Terrorists implicitly concede that the government has higher humanitarian standards than their own, irrespective of the rhetoric that justifies their actions, for terrorism is only "successful" if the target is more concerned about the welfare of the victims than is the terrorist. This is a paradox for those terrorising "evil" governments.

The government is constrained by public reaction to its behaviour during a hostage incident:

- If it gives in to save lives, it cannot protect society from terrorist violence.
- If it refuses any deals with the terrorists, resulting in harm to the victims, it fails to protect citizens from the terrorists and loses face.
- If it attempts a physical rescue which also harms the victims, it is shown to be incompetent.

The government, not the terrorists, is usually put on trial by the media.

The INTERESTS of the victims (survival) differ from those of both the terrorists and the government. Behaviour conducive to survival is also their best STRATEGY – a victim has no option. Advice about handling the role of victim includes the following:

- Keep a low profile.
- Show no dissent.
- Do not argue with their beliefs.
- Do not attack their beliefs.
- Express no views.
- Show no impatience at all.

If the hostage group is small enough (a dozen or less), there is a possibility of the "Stockholm Syndrome" emerging, which is a bonding relationship between the terrorists and the victims. This can save lives. But making friends with the terrorists in a larger group is dangerous if the situation turns sour. They may need somebody to execute to increase their commitment, and if they shoot their friends, clearly they will shoot hostile strangers.

Choosing to negotiate with hostage-takers involves the following objectives:

- The release of the victims unharmed.
- The failure of the terrorists to extract CONCESSIONS of substance.
- Dissuasion of imitators.

Prevention of terrorism is better than curing it, but failing prevention, what are the options?

The terrorists reinforce commitment by threatening to kill hostages. Initially, they set out their demands (which if ludicrously high imply irrational and probably unstable people, and if very low imply media manipulators). They demand to communicate with high officials, they demand publicity, they set deadlines. Either the deadlines are extended or they implement their threats.

Governments should leave negotiations to the security forces. It is best that the official in communication with the terrorists is, or is believed to be, of lowly rank. TIME is required to find out about the hostage-takers (to choose the most appropriate psychological approach) and to plan intervention by force.

The terrorists do not know for certain which policy the government is pursuing, so they impose short DEADLINES. They are constrained by the fact that shooting victims reduces the value of their threats (and gives the security forces a publicly acceptable reason for intervening by force). Tactics include:

- using time and isolation in tandem to undermine the terrorists' resolve to continue;
- doing nothing in a hurry, no matter what the THREAT, right from the start;
- doing everything possible to increase the feeling of normality in the immediate vicinity (do not close the airport – its continued functioning helps to undermine the terrorists' feeling of self-importance).

Here the media could help (but seldom do). Mentioning the

incident on occasional bulletins would help, rather than saturation coverage (not mentioning it at all for a day or so would be better).

High-level condemnation of the incident in public undermines the ploy of isolation, and senior ministers visiting the scene is utterly counterproductive.

In summary:

- Isolate the incident.
- Downplay its significance.
- Curtail (by self-denial) media coverage.
- Engage in negotiations at a low level.
- Make no moves in response to acts of violence.
- Maintain flexibility of means to achieve firmly set goals.

Remember: Winning a hostage crisis is seldom an option (the fact that it occurs is a victory for the terrorists). Your overall OBJECTIVE is to minimise the costs of concluding it without encouraging repetition.

Hotel purchase

Valuations of hotels are based on their income-earning capacities. One guide is the annual turnover (GROSS if selling; NET of taxes if buying). Turnover shows the recent trade of the hotel – what it actually does – not what it could do under your management. If there are unusual considerations producing recent turnover, these influence the PRICE.

If buying a hotel from a conglomerate, be wary of inflated turnover figures. Other divisions of the conglomerate could be under instruction to use the hotel services. Once sold to you, these purchases are no longer available.

When buying a hotel from a liquidator, be wary of the current trading accounts. The liquidator keeps the hotel open to sell it as a "going concern", and therefore slashes all expenditures to the bone. This reduces the cost of sales, and makes the potential profit look better than it is. Repairs and maintenance, even cleaning, can be suspended for a short period.

Base your OFFER price on annual turnover plus stock at valuation (SAV). If you do not want the stock, or any part of it (check all sell-by dates on booze and supplies), separate it out and require its disposal. Consider changing brewers to avoid paying for unsold previous stocks.

Try for contingency pricing if you doubt the figures.

If there are disposables (valuable furniture, valuable paintings, vases and clocks, spare land, spare buildings, associated fishing rights), can you sell them to reduce the cost of purchase? (Do not disclose your intentions; the seller could apply your ideas.)

Hustle close

A pressure ploy.

- The plane is leaving right now. It costs 4oz of gold for the last seat, or you learn Arabic.
- You know you'll never get a better deal than this one. If you don't take it right now, I'll ring off and call my LAWYERS.

Counter: Compare the OFFER against your options. If better, take it; if worse, do not (see BATNA).

If

A negotiator's most useful two-letter word. All PROPOSALS should start with "if" to tell them what they must do for you if you are to do something for them. If they reject your conditions you are free to amend, postpone, or withdraw your proposal.

"I'm only a simple grocer"

A disarming ploy to relax negotiators into indiscretions about their OBJECTIVES, tactics and hidden intentions. You think you are dealing with a novice because he or she claims to be "only a simple grocer", but in reality you are dealing with the owner of the world's largest grocery chain.

"I'm sorry, I've made a mistake"

A seller's ploy, close to the ETHICS border. A seller calls you back and apologises because she or he has made a mistake in the arithmetic of the order you placed. Instead of the products costing $4.55 each, they are listed in the catalogue at $4.95 each. The mistake was revealed when she placed your order for 1,000 units. She cannot sell them at $4.55 as her boss will not authorise the order. Her explanation is punctured with profuse apologies.

If you believe the seller to be genuine, you agree to the higher PRICE. If you do not, you cancel the order. This depends on how large the price mistake was compared with the total price, and how easy it is to find another seller. Usually buyers succumb, albeit reluctantly, to the ploy.

"Imperial" preference clauses

A BID ploy in which a bidder gains the right to bid last against the competition's prices and wins the contract by dipping a few percent below the lowest disclosed best PRICE.

If the buyer seeks bids when a preferred bidder has this right and does not inform all bidders that this arrangement is in place, it is unethical; if the bidder informs potential bidders that a preferred bidder has this right, no sensible bidder would take the trouble or expense to bid. It may be acceptable if the preferred bidder bids blind, and then only if its blind-bid price is within 3–5% of the lowest competitor would it win the contract.

Remedy: Ask if there is a preferred bidder with imperial preferences.

Imports

Without which we would be poorer (see EXPORTS).

Issues to negotiate with your supplier (the exporting company) include the following:

- Who bears the foreign exchange RISK?
- Who bears the cost of credit?
- Which PRICE prevails – ex-works; cost, insurance and freight (CIF); free on board (FOB)?
- How is the exporter paid?

Incentive

Motivating by carrot. Offer an incentive for measurable performance and people respond. Supplying incentive gifts (a euphemism for expensive staff presents) is a thriving business.

Indemnity 1

Expensive to buy; risky to do without.

Your professional advice puts you at RISK if somebody fouls up acting upon it. Indemnity insurance protects you against malpractice claims.

The premiums are high because malpractice awards are high; because they are high they are rife; they are rife because claimants are imaginative; claimants are imaginative because LAWYERS encourage claims to increase the awards; to reduce the awards insurers face high costs; because of the awards and high costs to insurers, the premiums are high.

The concept of unlimited liability for professional advisers was meant to concentrate their minds on the advisability of proffering advice without the greatest of due care and attention.

Indemnity 2

Tough distrust indeed; close cousin of WARRANTY.

You agree to "fully, promptly and effectively indemnify (the other party) against all costs, demands, actions, claims, liabilities and expenses (including but not limited to legal costs, losses and damages directly or indirectly relating to, resulting from or arising out of any breach of your warranties or undertakings or any negligent act or omission in connection with this AGREEMENT".

Indemnities are not to be treated lightly (they bankrupt the careless) because they usually survive the termination of an agreement. Only the super-rich or governments can afford to ignore the negotiation of indemnities. The rest of us must read them carefully, toughening them on the seller when we are buying, softening them when we are selling. Signing them casually is not an option.

Information

Can help or hinder your negotiation.

Information can be valuable when you discover how badly they need your co-operation. Conversely, disclosing your needs can damage your bank balance.

Inhibitions

Concerns that prevent you agreeing to a PROPOSAL. You must decide whether to present your inhibitions openly to the other side and require that they be addressed in their proposals, or leave them unexpressed while presenting proposals that address them. This saves revealing your prejudices.

LISTENING to what people say reveals their inhibitions:

- They do not TRUST you.
- They are worried about precedent.
- They need to be paid quickly.
- They want to be more selective than the law allows (sexism, racism, ageism, and so on).
- They are frightened of publicity.
- They do not know if it works.

Your proposals should address their inhibitions.

Integrative bargaining

Searching for solutions to problems where the negotiators have compatible INTERESTS.

By emphasising the commonality of interests in CONFLICT situations, integrative bargaining can reformulate distributive ZERO-SUM disputes into integrative NON-ZERO-SUM possibilities.

Integrative bargaining can lead to PROBLEM SOLVING.

Considerable TRUST in both you and the process is required (earned not assumed).

A mixture of integrative and DISTRIBUTIVE BARGAINING is more likely to be successful than an approach based totally on one or the other.

Interest rate

The PRICE of money. This varies widely. It can:

- cover for the opportunity cost of money (how much you can get in an alternative lending activity);
- cover for the RISK involved;
- reflect its scarcity value for you (how badly do you want the money?).

Interests

Why you prefer some things to others. Your interests motivate your wants. Interests may be hidden because you are:

- unaware of them;
- embarrassed by them;
- confusing them with your wants.

To uncover interests, ask why they want what they are demanding. Can you meet their interests in some other way?

When our interests are in conflict with our feelings we face a difficult choice.

Internet negotiation

Online negotiation is becoming more common and in the process creating some new solutions to old problems.

The main new problem is the impersonal context of online

communication. Messages seem harsher on the phone, in writing and in e-mails. Without visual contact, preferably face-to-face and not just by teleconferencing, many non-verbal clues, which normally assist mutual understanding and are activated informally outside the negotiation room, are missed. Negotiating by telephone (the original 19th-century internet) has long been widespread in many businesses, including in dealing rooms for foreign exchange, company shares and finance. Online exchanges have added a new dimension to this familiar activity.

One old problem of face-to-face negotiation is the dominance effect of (mainly male) status: one or two people do all the talking, initiate OFFERS and demands, and take responsibility for movement or the lack of it. Online communication eliminates this effect far more than the telephone has done, because the telephone reveals the male/female persona. This and the sender's corporate status may be completely masked by an e-mail user name (you could be receiving instructions from the CEO or the mailroom clerk).

Using a teleconference to negotiate requires synchronous availability of all parties, which may be awkward across different time zones, at short notice and over weekends (especially where local "weekends" differ). E-mail contact is asynchronous (although we expect early responses) and much can be communicated and stored in one message, without repeatedly and fruitlessly telephoning someone who is away from their desk or relying on the vagaries of when they check their voicemail.

E-mail may reproduce harmful impersonal effects in the negotiating climate, leading to BLAME CYCLES, DEADLOCK, ESCALATION, MANIPULATIVE PLOYS and aggressive stances. Rapid responses and counter-responses easily lead to the mutual attribution of negative motives and personal denigration (known as "flaming" exchanges).

It is best to make use of a variety of media to conduct negotiations: some by personal face-to-face contact to establish a visual relationship; some by telephone; some by e-mail; and some by printed documents. If personal relationships are downplayed through overabundant use of online exchanges only, the transaction side of the relationship will be enhanced and might even dominate all exchanges. A step towards reconstituting a business relationship would include greater use of telephone contact and, perhaps, occasional personal visits.

The most well-known online application is in the AUCTION business. Other applications include:

- Procurement websites, where business-to-business transactions, mainly in basic industrial materials (metals, oil and gas, standard components, chemicals, electricity, cement, plastics, motor vehicles and such like), take place. Initially, this allegedly cuts up to 20% of procurement costs, including the costs of face-to-face negotiations with suppliers.

- Legal and insurance services where the parties can elect to "negotiate" online. Variations of a generic model exist in the United States and the UK. Basically, the insurer and the plaintiff's lawyer each post up to three settlement PROPOSALS on the system. If any of the offers and demands overlap within an agreed range, a settlement, which the parties have pre-agreed to accept, is announced at a median point by the system's software. This has a potential for use in divorce settlements.

- Civil action claims by the parties' LAWYERS. The parties save time and cost in the usual prolonged exchange of correspondence, face-to-face meetings, mutual denials and accusations of culpability, which often are not related to the real "value" of the claim. If there is a FAILURE TO AGREE, the parties may elect to revert to traditional negotiation or go to trial.

Interpersonal orientation

Psychological insight into how people interact. Negotiators operate along a continuum. They have a high interpersonal orientation if they are responsive to other people. They have a low interpersonal orientation if they prefer to be uninvolved with what is happening to others.

Two negotiators both with high interpersonal orientation:

■ engage in co-operative behaviour;
■ are likely to solve problems;
■ have warm personal relations.

Negotiators with a low interpersonal orientation:

■ aim to gain as much as they can without consideration of the other's behaviour;
■ do not take anything personally;
■ believe that the balance of POWER pushes others to behave competitively or co-operatively (out of confidence or desperation);
■ work for their own INTERESTS;
■ do not react to others' behaviours;
■ exploit a co-operative stance;
■ expect the other negotiators to look after their own interests and to be the best judge of them;
■ are not the best team members for a delicate and sensitive negotiation;
■ are useful in the early stages of a difficult negotiation (ceasefire, arms control, exchange of prisoners);
■ are not useful if relationships need to be warmed;
■ offend some negotiators and cause breakdowns that have nothing to do with the substantive issues.

Two negotiators with low interpersonal orientations:

■ aim to maximise their own interests;
■ delay settlement because their moves are based only on self-interest;

■ do not generate bonds of TRUST.

The two interpersonal orientations produce four personality styles:

■ Competitive stylists, who consider negotiation as a contest, often gladiatorial and certainly adversarial ("what I gain you lose").
■ Avoiders, who prefer not to negotiate at all and avoid the stress or embarrassment they feel by postponing decision-making and making excuses.
■ Accommodators, who are unassertive and prefer to go along with the other party's suggestions, and go out of their way to be liked rather than be confrontational.
■ Collaborators, who seek the proverbial WIN-WIN solution to any problem and prefer joint gains to one-sided "winning", and seek to increase the pie rather than fight over a fixed one.

It is pointless to ask which style produces the best negotiators, as all personality types have to negotiate at some time or other. Each may shine in some negotiation circumstances and fail miserably in others. If personality is the independent driver of negotiating behaviour and it takes nine serious psychological tests lasting several hours to uncover a negotiator's personality, the personality approach – determining the other party's personality and adapting your behaviour accordingly – is impractical while negotiating. Moreover, if through negotiation training a person can learn to override their personality, how significant is personality?

Intimidation

Can be overt (bullying, gangsterism) or covert (self-induced). Covert intimidation is more widespread but hardly noticeable. It works almost entirely through your own mind.

Covert intimidation operates through the power of suggestion.

It is the ultimate untested assumption. People covertly intimidate because it works.

Intimidator

You may never know you have been intimidated covertly. Well-worn intimidators include the following:

- Uncomfortable seating, lower down than the intimidator's.
- Poorly positioned seating, such as in a draught, facing the sun or its reflection, or in front of an open door through which other people can hear your conversation.
- You are kept waiting.

  During the negotiation intimidators may:

- take phone calls, speak to secretaries and colleagues and look at their watches;
- tell somebody they will be free in a few minutes when you have just started;
- complain about your products or services as well as your company;
- praise the competition and appear to know all your rivals by their first names (they keep forgetting yours);
- not appear to be paying attention or showing interest in anything you say;
- not read your literature, not answer QUESTIONS or state their needs, and generally appear to be indifferent.

Intimidators are not rude, they are at work on your PERCEPTIONS. They aim to force you to move further towards their targets than you intended.

Karrass, Chester

A star performer and doyen of the approach known as STREET-WISE NEGOTIATION, now retired. He was head of procurement at Hughes Aircraft for many years and knew more than most about the practice of negotiation.

Kidnap negotiation

Kidnappers coerce their targets by threatening to harm their victims. Kidnapping poses different problems from those of HOSTAGE taking:

- The kidnappers' lair is not known.
- The police are not deployed outside it.
- The kidnappers choose and prepare their location.
- The kidnappers choose when to communicate with the target.
- The police cannot manipulate the environment to isolate the kidnappers.
- The kidnappers do not seek publicity.
- The kidnappers can rest at will.
- The kidnappers choose whether to continue extortion or quit (about 20% of kidnap victims are killed).

The target must decide whether to involve the authorities or to meet the kidnappers' demands. Whereas an individual can be intimidated into ignoring a crime, the state cannot.

Kidnappers are vulnerable during the handover of the ransom because they have to reveal where and when to do so. Laws prohibit the paying of ransom and the entire assets of a target can be frozen to prevent it. These laws can be circumvented if the target has resources outside their jurisdiction and can pay without revealing the details to the authorities.

Targets have to be sure they are dealing with the people who actually hold the victim, because some callers will be bogus (you could use code words). If interlopers have solved the handover problem but do not hold the victim, you could be paying for nothing. Evidence that the victim is alive or the property is intact (for example, photographs containing today's newspaper) can be demanded in return for co-operating to pay the ransom, but most evidence is unreliable and, anyway, may be refused. Never pay cash for "proof of life". It becomes another means of extracting money from the target.

However, the main kidnap insurers employ professional experts to negotiate in kidnap negotiation who are often considerably more experienced in this line of work than the regular authorities. Professionals abide by two main rules: the release of the victim unharmed (the principal objective) and payment of the minimum tariff to the kidnappers. They do not get involved in rescue attempts or in entrapments by the authorities, although they work closely with the police. Their client's INTERESTS are paramount.

Killer line

The killer lines that put you on the spot include:

- You'll have to do better than that.
- Give me your best PRICE.

One sentence gets them a major CONCESSION, so they will probably try a few more "killers" to see just how soft you are on price. In fact, you may be bidding downwards against yourself.

Counter: Seek more information.

- What other PROPOSALS have they received?
- Is it apples and pears?
- If they have a better price, why don't they take it?

Either there is something in your proposal they like, which means it is worth its price, or they are fishing with a price challenge. Think about your reaction to killer lines.

Killer questions

QUESTIONS to put you on the spot. Answer yes or no and you could be in trouble.

For example: "Is that your final OFFER?" Yes ends the negotiation. No tells the other negotiators that you have other (better for them) PROPOSALS.

Their next question is going to be: "Well, what is your final offer? Is that proposal negotiable?" Yes opens the negotiation on your next proposal. No ends the negotiation.

Counter: "My proposal is based on the circumstances as I understand them at present, but I am always willing to listen to constructive suggestions that will improve the acceptability of my proposal."

Krunch

Or the Karrass Krunch, as Chester KARRASS called it. The buyer tells the seller: "You have to do much better than that." It works because sellers build slack into their PRICES and open with their FIRST OFFER, which is seldom their last offer. For sellers' counters, see NOAH'S ARK.

Last clear chance

A method to apportion blame for an incident. Even if both parties contribute to it, the one with the last clear chance to prevent it is culpable. If you have the last clear chance to avert the incident (STRIKE, failure to supply), you have the unenviable choice of backing off or causing it.

Law

Best observed, especially when inconvenient.

The rule of law is preferred to the rule of men. For every victim of an unjust law, there are many more victims of unjust conduct. Without the rule of law:

- contracts would be unenforceable;
- property rights would be meaningless;
- promises need not be kept;
- THREATS would be arbitrary;
- lives could be in jeopardy.

Lawyers

Regular negotiators – with other lawyers. They usually act as AGENTS of non-lawyers, creating PRINCIPAL–AGENT PROBLEMS. The spectre of a resort to litigation – and the mutual calculus of the probability of victory or defeat in court – drives lawyers to favour settlement or otherwise. If each client's lawyers assure their PRINCIPAL of victory, either they don't know their law or the client has been economical with the facts.

Most disputants settle "on the courthouse steps", sometimes because there are no cheap lawyers and costs mount when trial lawyers and barristers join the payroll, and sometimes because the lawyers do know their law and become suspicious of their client's facts. It is better to use lawyers only to negotiate a settlement. Even if it is less than fair or full justice, it is always cheaper than going to trial.

Lease

An alternative to ownership.

Consider the following points when negotiating a lease AGREEMENT:

- Who is the agreement between?
- Is there a declaration of non-nominee status? If falsely declared, the property reverts with no compensation and without prejudice to money owed.
- Who is guaranteeing the lessee's obligations? If the lessee fails to meet obligations, reversion clause applies.
- What exactly is being leased?
- How much is the RENT?
- When is it paid (in advance or arrears, monthly, quarterly)?
- Is there a premium and on what basis? For the "fixtures and fittings", for the "availability" of the lease?
- How long is the lease for?
- When does it commence?
- Can it be extended and on whose initiative?
- When are RENT REVIEWS scheduled and are they upward only?
- What criteria apply – cost of living, valuation and yield of similar properties?
- How are disputes settled?
- Is there a "rent-free" period and for how long?

- Who pays other charges during this period?
- What service charges is the lessee liable for?
- Who pays the rates/service charges?
- Is it a "full repairs and insurance" lease?
- What access does the lessor have for inspections?
- Who specifies extent of repairs and choice of contractor?
- Can the lessee sublet with the lessor's consent ("not unreasonably withheld")?
- Within what duration of the lease (rent-review period only)?
- Can the lessee assign lease with or without the lessor's consent?
- On what terms can the lessee surrender the lease?
- Who pays legal costs of the transaction?
- What obligations does the tenant have to planning regulations?
- If new regulations apply during the tenancy, who pays for them?
- What obligations does the tenant have to the building's fixtures and fittings and to their good care and upkeep?
- What notification must the lessee give of intentions to make any alterations to the building?
- What regulations must the lessee apply? These may include:
  - fire certificates;
  - prohibitions on storing dangerous or toxic chemicals;
  - prohibitions on specified dangerous or illegal (or disreputable?) activities;
  - compliance with all laws on occupation and use;
  - official cubic space per person employed;
  - refraining from causing a nuisance or obstruction of any kind and suchlike.
- Reversion clause to apply for serious or persistent minor breaches at the lessor's discretion.

Lendability factor

A subjective judgment (by the lender, not yourself) of the following:

- Your character: are you to be trusted with their money?
- Your record: what your recent past shows.
- Your propositions: what the money is to be used for (how it increases your NET worth).
- Your terms: what is in it for the lender.

Letter of credit

Facilitates foreign trade; terms are negotiable.

If exporting, require the importer to open a credit with your bank for the value of the goods, CIF or FOB, with the following features:

- Confirmed: importer's bank guarantees payment on production of appropriate shipping documents.
- Irrevocable: prevents importer refusing payment on a pretext.
- Transferable: enables you to endorse it for other transactions.
- Divisible: for part-payments on other deals.

If importing, require the exporter to accept a letter of credit (LOC).

- Make it payable when the goods have passed your inspection (is revocable).
- Trade this for transferability and divisibility, which are direct benefits to the payee.

Practice varies and reflects the balance of POWER. The wording of a LOC is crucial, and should be scrutinised carefully. A glance at disputes in case law over LOCs should keep you awake at night.

Level up the work, level down the price

No two BIDS are exactly the same, except through collusion. Each includes different commitments and features.

Select the commitments and features that you prefer. This is your "levelled-up work specification". Ask the suppliers to re-offer the levelled-up specification. Ask the suppliers to re-offer the levelled-up specification at or below the lowest priced quotation. This is your "levelled-down PRICE".

Some suppliers might not re-bid. Others might re-bid and move up on price. If anybody re-bids and meets the levelled-down price, consider awarding them the contract (but beware of BLOCKING BIDS).

Leverage

BARGAINING power. It is important to know what leverage you have, even if you choose not to apply it.

Almost anything that you have discretion over gives you leverage. Who has leverage?

- Air traffic controllers at holiday time.
- Construction workers when a project is time-critical.
- Exhibition workers when it is due to open.
- Stage hands just before the show.
- Advertisers when TV channels have spare slots.
- TV channels when prime-time slots are full.

Counters: Not easy, otherwise it is not leverage. Raise the stakes:

- Sack the air traffic controllers.
- Cancel the event.
- Lock out strikers for twice as long as they strike.
- Ban advertisers for six months.
- Switch channels, or media.

Lower the stakes:

- Reward negotiators who do not apply leverage unfairly.
- Negotiate other than when leverage can be applied.
- Do not exploit your own leverage.
- Reward advertisers who pay full rates with prime-time preference slots.
- Reward TV channels that give preference with off-peak bookings.

Lifeboat clause

When you need a lifeboat, you need a lifeboat. For protection when buying add:

This offer is contingent on the veracity of all statements made by the seller in respect of the proposed sale, including all statements regarding performance, quality, availability and specifications, and approval of the buyer of all matters relevant to the purchase, whether presently known or not, and any other material facts that may affect the buyer's interests.

You now have an exit should you find it in your INTERESTS to jump into a lifeboat.

Lifetime costs

Forget them at your peril. Remember the acquisition cost is only part of the PRICE. How much does it cost to maintain the purchased item or service?

Linking

Opens up BARGAINING possibilities.

You are presented with a list of demands, or an OFFER with

more than one element. Do you deal with each issue separately by treating each one as a distinct mini-negotiation, or link them together on the basis that "nothing is agreed until everything is agreed"?

Separating the issues has an advantage: it narrows down the remaining items in dispute. This blocks off obstructive ploys by parties who hold out for CONCESSIONS in one area favourable to them for agreement in other areas favourable to them.

Separating the issues has disadvantages, however. The outstanding issues are normally contentious (that is why they are outstanding). This leaves little room for movement by the parties. The settled issues may have been settled too quickly, curtailing opportunities for additional movement on them. By separating the issues, you could be restricting yourself when you come to deal with the contentious items.

By linking the issues you negotiate where you can get an AGREEMENT, but any agreement is "subject to agreement on all the issues". Linking is much more complex than single issue BARGAINING. SUMMARISING skills are valuable at any time, but they are at a premium in a linked negotiation.

Liquidity

Highly desirable when you need it, expensive when you do not.

Assets have varying degrees of liquidity. Cash has instant liquidity, but:

- it does not earn interest;
- holding large sums in cash is expensive in your forgone earnings;
- it is risky (thieves, fire, flood, carelessness and prodigality).

Money in a bank with instant access during banking hours is as good as cash. ATMs (automatic teller machines) give 24 hours' liquidity.

Listening

The least successful skill of the below-average negotiator.

It could be the only CONCESSION the other negotiators require. They want somebody to listen to their views, respect them and take account of them, and do not expect more than that.

The message sent is often not the one that is received. People are poor listeners. Even if the message is heard clearly, recall deteriorates rapidly as TIME passes.

Listening to what a negotiator says is hard work. Experiments show how difficult it is to recall accurately even vivid messages, let alone routine ones.

Here are some tips to improve your listening skills.

- Ask QUESTIONS for clarification.
- Summarise the statements to the satisfaction of the speaker.
- Don't interrupt.
- Avoid composing your rejection of what they are saying before they finish.
- Cease anticipating what they are about to say (you miss the surprises).
- Don't judge the message by the messenger.
- Treat their statements with respect.
- Avoid reacting emotionally to views you find distasteful or otherwise disagreeable.

Here are some tips to improve the other negotiators' listening skills.

- Speak clearly and for short periods only.
- Summarise your points.
- Answer questions briefly.
- Avoid diluting your stronger points with weaker points that divert attention from your main message.

Loan

Against COLLATERAL, a loan can be worthwhile.

It makes sense to borrow other people's money for wealth-creating purposes only. It never makes sense to borrow, or to lend, for income.

Lock-out

Supposedly management's answer to a STRIKE. The company refuses work for its employees until certain conditions are met, such as a return to "normal working" or a willingness to undertake specified duties.

Disruptive union tactics can be countered by a lock-out. Unions usually pursue disruptive tactics because:

- they are not sure of the support for an all-out strike;
- they can levy those continuing to work to pay the wages of those sent home without pay for carrying out union instructions;
- they can prolong a dispute for months, causing more problems for the company than for union members.

Should the company impose costs on the employees by sending the entire workforce home? Yes, if this is likely to force a more realistic negotiating stance on the union. No, if the dispute slides into intransigence (see MARTYRDOM).

Alternatively, can the system cope by adapting to the loss of key staff and thus isolate those whose labour has been withdrawn? Any levy costs imposed by the union on those not striking weakens the support of the rest.

Lose–lose

It happens. Neither party can find a compromise, either because they insist on the other moving only, or because there is no settlement range in their respective positions.

By insisting on winning, they both lose.

Major sacrifice gambit

A ploy that manipulates the PERCEPTIONS of the other negotiator. Having decided on a traded CONCESSION, you refer to its "significance" and build it up as a major concession as credibly as you can.

If they believe you, they might offer another concession on another issue. Suggest an area where they can compensate you for your "heroic" sacrifice.

Management fees

An alternative to the ownership of capital assets, which are at RISK of expropriation, destruction, or deterioration.

Propose a contract to manage assets on their owner's behalf, or to provide a service that the client prefers not to supply itself. Fee income is calculated on "what the MARKET will bear", consistent with a minimum level to cover actual costs.

The benefits include:

- not having large capital projects at RISK;
- not having to fund them.

Your net earnings can be equivalent to your earnings from owning and operating the capital commitment.

From the owner's point of view the drawbacks include:

- vulnerability to the managers setting a fee structure which you cannot audit for value;
- where the negotiated fee exceeds the expected profit from the assets, you reduce funds available from investment;

- where you reduce the negotiated fee, the professional managers might depart, leaving inefficiently managed assets.

The owner's STRATEGY is to acquire local expertise in managing local assets through requiring the managing company to train local people to become professional managers to replace the management company at some date in the future, and to reduce fees towards competitive rates by issuing tenders for the management contract (especially at renewal dates) to local and international management companies.

Mandate

Defines and limits your authority.

Discretion is a heavy but avoidable responsibility. If you exceed your mandate your deal could be repudiated (and those responsible could be "reassigned").

Employees limit the discretion of their representatives by mandating them not to accept any PROPOSAL without their approval, and not to accept anything less than the mandated demand. This is often a COMMITMENT PLOY rather than an immovable stance.

How might you handle a mandate demand? Not by conceding it, unless you want to receive more mandate demands (see SKINNER'S PIGEON). If you believe it is a commitment ploy, do not challenge the commitment; they might demonstrate how strongly they feel committed. If the mandate is the true wish of the employees, threat their feelings firmly, through gently, and with a regard to your INTERESTS.

Not all mandate demands survive the first refusal.

Manipulative ploys

There is a considerable market in offering advice on how to manipulate during negotiation. This is often presented, craftily, under the phoney guise of "how to stop other people manipulating" (but "first, we must learn how manipulators manipulate us decent folk").

All manipulative ploys divide into three types:

- dominance
- shaping
- closing

Manipulators use dominance ploys by.

- insisting on preconditions;
- declaring some issues are non-negotiable;
- attempting to decide on the AGENDA, its order and timing;
- behaving in an aggressive red BEHAVIOURAL STYLE;
- threatening sanctions;
- displaying calculated scepticism about you, your product, your business and your performance;
- being difficult negotiators.

Manipulators use shaping ploys by:

- playing tough guy/nice guy;
- using SALAMI;
- using ADD-ON;
- trying the MOTHER HUBBARD;
- trying the RUSSIAN FRONT.

Manipulators use closing ploys by:

- demanding that you split the difference;
- claiming it is "now or never";
- setting phoney deadlines;
- threatening with the OR ELSE close;
- pretending to WALK OUT.

If you know what the manipulators are up to, it is easier to counter them (every ploy has at least one counter) or to ignore them (any ploy is weakened by being ignored). A manipulative ploy identified is a ploy neutered.

All ploys aim to manipulate your PERCEPTIONS and EXPECTATIONS. Manipulation works best when you do not realise you are being manipulated.

Market

An unintended human creation that does not discriminate on the basis of sex, religion, status, race, political belief, location, history or intention. No matter who you are, how you feel, how anybody else feels about you or what you do, the market is neutral.

The market:

- processes information about PRICES;
- can be extensive in a global sense or localised;
- signals discrepancies in wants and the means to meet them, and does so without central or any other kind of direction;
- is robust regarding interference (though not indefinitely);
- is suppressible only in the short term;
- is pervasive across language, cultural and ethnic barriers.

The nature of markets creates the need for negotiation, for although the market signals a price, that price is the result of infinite adjustments by people to their PERCEPTIONS of demand and supply. Many of these adjustments are contradictory. People:

- sell when they should hold on;
- buy when they should desist;
- do neither when they should do both.

The constant adjustment of the market, its impermanence for more than a moment and its uncertainty about the future, make negotiating its ideal instrument.

Martyrdom

Never underestimate the ability of people to perform acts that are detrimental to their best INTERESTS. Do not assume that people rationally calculate the net benefits of a course of action.

Negotiators can react irrationally, even suicidally, to change. They know that they are going to lose, but their defiance is fed by their emotions.

Martyrdom comforts the defiant, the desperate and the dedicated, which for them far outweighs their sacrifice.

Threatening martyrs plays into their hands; they receive a new lease of life and public sympathy, instead of rejection as a clown.

Martyrs can be exasperating, dangerous and expensive.

Mediation

Shares a blurred boundary between ARBITRATION and negotiation. Negotiators in DEADLOCK might still want to find a settlement, yet neither of them can find a way to move. A mediator seeks a "safe" way for each side to make movement.

Unlike an arbitrator, a mediator does not enforce movement. The mediator first identifies and then informs each negotiator that there is a possibility of movement.

The mediator establishes whether there is a settlement range of which the parties are presently unaware. The mediator is not concerned with the justice of each negotiator's position, how "fair" or "reasonable" it is, or whether it corresponds to the "facts". However, the mediator may caution the negotiators that their PROPOSAL contains serious obstacles to its acceptance, but it remains the negotiators' responsibility whether to pursue a proposal.

Mediators must:

■ take firm charge of the process of dispute settlement;

- be totally indifferent to the settlement;
- not deliberate or judge the merits of the issues;
- set the rules of the debate;
- not permit interruption of what one person says ("your turn comes later");
- permit any option from the list of possible solutions ("no option is agreed or rejected just because it is discussed");
- insist on no negotiation until all the views of each side have been expressed.

The mediator asks each negotiator privately to verify the basis of their facts and claims and to reveal confidentially the basis upon which they consider their proposed solutions would be acceptable.

Memorandum of understanding

Drawn up to commit the parties loosely before the details are agreed. A memorandum of understanding (MOU) outlines the mutual understanding of the negotiators about their intentions to proceed to an AGREEMENT without finally binding them into an irreversible relationship.

Always insert a sentence saying "This MOU is subject to final contract" and see that it appears in all correspondence referring to the MOU.

Minimum order ploy

Enhances the value of an order for the seller. Examples include the following:

- We only sell these in packs of six.
- If we represent you in the purchase of the building, we must also act as letting agents if you acquire it.

Counter: Test their seriousness by your certain choice of the alternative of no order at all.

Minutes

Minutes record:

- who was present during the negotiation;
- when and where the negotiation took place;
- brief notes on the AGENDA;
- summaries of each negotiator's main views;
- commitments to look at specific topics;
- PROPOSALS that are made;
- anything that is agreed.

Minuting a discussion is not easy even if you are neutral; when you are one of the players it is difficult to do to the complete satisfaction of the other negotiators. Do not succumb to the temptation to "bend" the minute to suit your own INTERESTS. They may fail to notice the alteration, but they are less likely not to notice its consequences. It is interesting that most mistakes in minutes benefit the side that wrote the minutes.

Mother Hubbard

A PRICE pressure ploy implying that the "cupboard is bare". The buyer can challenge the seller's price as follows.

- Assert that you desire to buy, but convince them that your budget does not allow you to buy at the price they have quoted. Support this with evidence (for example, MINUTES of the budget meeting, written instructions).
- Block off all attempts to restructure your budget by running it over two periods, virement across different headings, instalments and "creative accounting".

- Place the onus of finding a way of reducing the price on the seller.

Close to a sale they will search for ways of coming down to your budget. Some of the changes will be:

- cosmetic but nevertheless valuable to you;
- "creative accounting" (in their accounts not yours);
- tangible to you (shifting the money to after-sales costs;
- a straight cut in price.

How far you place your Mother Hubbard below their quoted price is a matter of judgment: too far and they break off; too close and you pay more than you need to (though any price cut is better than none).

Counter: Difficult if the cupboard really is bare. Try detailed questioning of their budget process, and uncover where the authority lies to change it. It is better to be over their alleged budget because you have priced the "extras" as ADD-ONS than over it with everything priced on an inclusive basis.

Motivation

Other people have baser motives than ourselves. This harmless delusion becomes dangerous when we act as if other negotiators respond only to the motivations we ascribe to them.

Ascribed motive	Competitive action	Co-operative action
Fear	Threaten	Assure
Pride	Mock	Flatter
Hatred	Hate	Love
Loyalty	Exploit	Reward
Money	Minimise	Maximise
Love	Withhold	Requite
Desire	Frustrate	Satisfy

Ascribed motive	Competitive action	Co-operative action
Jealousy	Excite	Calm
Ambition	Block	Assist

To assume that money is the only motivator of all employees ignores a whole range of other motivators, some of which, if recognised and attended to, might be cheaper that an elaborate pay reward system.

MOU

See MEMORANDUM OF UNDERSTANDING.

Mutuality

A good test of the other negotiator's intentions.

If key clauses are written as ONE-WAY STREETS, be warned: they may be setting you up, or their LAWYERS are trying it on. Mutuality in commercial negotiations is based on mutual respect, evidenced by an intention not to impose onerous conditions and consequences on you without accepting the same conditions on themselves.

Remedy: insist on mutuality.

Mutuality principle

The union claims a mutual right with the management to decide on certain issues. Union STRATEGY is to widen the areas of MUTUALITY from conventional wages and working conditions to areas normally reserved as prerogatives of management.

Unions also seek to achieve mutuality on some older areas of managerial prerogatives, such as promotion, selection, hiring, discipline, firing and training.

Nn

Nash solution

An economist's model of the solution to the BARGAINING problem.

Nash showed that faced with a choice of achieving some minimum outcome (their "security level") and incrementally improving on that level by accommodating to each other, negotiators did best for each other when they maximised the product of their incremental utilities. Nash's solution, by ASSUMPTIONS, abstracts from the skills and bargaining POWER of each individual. It also ignores the process of negotiation. It is solely about the optimum outcome.

Need to know

Security in the negotiating team is a prudent precaution. Premature disclosure whether by accident or theft worsens your prospects of a deal.

Negotiating teams should take the following precautions:

- Prepare in secure premises.
- Adopt a numbering system for all documents and restrict their circulation.
- Brief senior personnel in person.
- Remember only the negotiators need to see the briefs and the crucial data.
- Shred all documents once they have been superseded (and delete computer files, wipe disks and memory sticks).
- Allow no work to be taken home or on foreign trips.

■ Enlist positive support for basic security measures from all the negotiators involved.
■ Screen the secretariat and the services people (cleaning company employees too).
■ Relieve colleagues with known personal problems of involvement in a stressful negotiation.

Needs theory

Meet a negotiator's needs and you are on your way towards agreement, says Gerard Nierenberg, who developed an approach that begins with Maslow's hierarchy of needs (see PSYCHOLOGY OF NEGOTIATION).

Nierenberg categorises six types of application to each hierarchy of need, ranked by the degree of control which negotiators may exercise over the outcome. These are as follows.

1   Negotiators working for the opposers' needs: assure, encourage, concede.
2   Negotiators letting the opposers work for their own needs: motivate, permit, challenge.
3   Negotiators working for the opposers' and their own needs: co-operate, compromise, recognise.
4   Negotiators working against their own needs: waive, relinquish, disavow.
5   Negotiators working against the opposers' needs: veto, embarrass, threaten.
6   Negotiators working against the opposers' and their own needs: thwart, renounce, withdraw.

Each need has an appropriate, or potential, tactic and can be applied to interpersonal, inter-organisational and diplomatic conflicts.

Negotiating language

Some types of language help a negotiation, particularly in the BARGAINING phase. "We require" is more assertive than "we would like" and it is more likely to get attention than a vague expression of desire.

Tell them what you want, and tell them what you are willing to TRADE with them to get it.

Assertive language	Weaker language
I require	I would like
I need	I wish
I must	I hope
I want	I fancy
I insist	I feel

Negotiating skill

What distinguishes the above-average negotiator from the rest? Studies of negotiators have identified some of the characteristics of above-average negotiators. If the difference in performance can be replicated with training and practice, below-average negotiators can improve their performance.

Neil Rackham and John Carlisle concluded that the differences in performance were sufficiently consistent as to be identified and run as a training programme. Broadly, above-average negotiators:

- Explore more options.
- Devote much more TIME to considering areas of potential agreement (though both spend most of their time considering their differences).
- Spend twice as much time considering long-term as opposed to short-term issues (though both spend over 90% of their time on the short-term issues).
- Set OBJECTIVES within a range rather than a fixed point.

- Leave open the order in which they consider the issues during face-to-face contact.
- Use far fewer irritators (self-praise for their own PROPOSALS), which do not persuade and are therefore counter-productive.
- Make far fewer instant counter-proposals.
- Initiate far fewer defend/attack spirals.
- Label their own behaviour before proceeding ("Could I ask a question?"), although when about to disagree, they give their reasons first and then state that they disagree.
- Test their understanding more often.
- Summarise more often.
- Ask many more QUESTIONS.
- Give more information about personal feelings.
- Refrain from diluting ARGUMENTS with weaker and more vulnerable statements.
- Review the events that had occurred during the negotiation.

Negotiating with yourself

A common enough activity. We perceive we are weaker than we really are and we lower our EXPECTATIONS. We anticipate how they are likely to react to our PROPOSALS, so we soften them. It is much more fruitful to negotiate with the other party than ourselves; they too may be negotiating with themselves.

Net

Always smaller than GROSS, so be careful when negotiators refer to net amounts.

The gross amount, less deductibles, equals the net amount. Deductibles are disputable. The share of a net sum, be it profit, income or interest, is of uncertain value to the receiver, and depends on the motives of the calculator. Offer net shares, but demand gross shares.

Nibble

Nibbling pays – sometimes.

Sellers nibble by overshipments (and charging for them) and undershipments (and charging for full shipments), by not performing fully, by shipping slightly inferior merchandise and by charging for "extras". Buyers nibble by late payments, taking discounts, requesting special deliveries, broken runs, special returns policies, and free training and consultancy. Chester KARRASS says: "If you can't get a dinner get a sandwich."

Nibbles add up: they are good for your cash flow. They also cause aggravation: they are not good for business relationships.

Remedy: Strict enforcement of contractual terms and, eventually, delisting of a supplier or customer

No come-backs

The truly one-off deal. No WARRANTIES, no promises, no returns and no responsibility for anything once the deal is concluded. It is *caveat emptor* (and *caveat vendor*). You live with what you bought, or without it, as the case may be.

No problem

A reckless CONCESSION.

Q: Can you deliver overnight?
A: No problem.
Q: We need 24-hour call-outs on this equipment.
A: No problem.

"No problem" concessions are wasted. They might be prepared to compensate generously, but you do not know if you do not try.

Put them on the spot.

Q: Are you saying that if we do deliver overnight you will award us the contract?

Q: If we can offer a 24-hour service, do we get the business?

No sale, no fee

A version of contingency pricing. Payment for services is based exclusively on results.

"No fee" could still involve costs (advertising and other expenses) even when no sale occurred. If a sale takes place, but the fee-earner was not responsible for the sale, do they still get a fee?

Noah's ark

A buyer's pressure ploy: "You'll have to do better than that because your rivals are quoting better prices than you are." It is almost always a BLUFF. It has been part of the buyer's repertoire of winning moves for so long that Noah let two of them on board.

Sometimes buyers do have a better PRICE, but more often they do not have comparable packages from the sellers (see APPLES AND PEARS).

- **Comparable packages but different prices.** If you drop your price, the buyer is better off by the difference and can induce your rival to follow suit against you (see DUTCH AUCTION).

- **Non-comparable packages and therefore non-comparable prices.** If you believe that the PROPOSALS are comparable and you reduce your price, the buyer is better off.

- **Rivals' prices are higher (or you believe them to be).** If you reduce your prices to defeat rivals (real or imagined), the buyer is better off.

Counters

- Question the buyer's comparisons.
- Refuse to react unless you can compare the quotes direct.
- Ask why the buyer is dealing with you if your rivals' quotes are better.

Non-verbal behaviour

55% of a negotiator's message is perceived non-verbally; only 7% depends on what is said and 38% on how it is said.

It is not that a single gesture reveals all but how gestures fit in with what we are trying to say. If they contradict our words, then the message received is different from the one sent.

- Crowding the private space of the other negotiator or pumping a stranger's handshake as if he were a long-lost friend can destroy the intended effect.
- Touching the face, rubbing the cheek, covering the mouth and suchlike can mean someone is being less than candid; it can also mean that they have an itch or they were eating garlic last night.
- Chin stroking can mean they are coming to a decision. It is not sensible to interrupt their thoughts at this point.
- If the other negotiator sits back, folds her arms and is about to say something, it is almost certainly going to be "no", so swift intervention to go over the positive points in your PROPOSAL might be helpful.
- Hands folded across the chest are defensive, suggesting that the other negotiator does not accept what you have said.

Non-verbal behaviour is underrated by some people and over-rated by others. A brilliantly manipulated message is unlikely to be successful if the content is unacceptable; and a badly sent message that would otherwise be acceptable could be rejected because the listener has grave doubts about your true intentions.

Non-zero sum

What you gain is not at my expense (see ZERO SUM). The sum of the positive gains is greater than zero.

Suppose you are negotiating several issues, such as:

- PRICE per unit;
- quantity to be delivered;
- when payment is to be made;
- specification;
- policy on returns of defective units;

Your INTERESTS as the buyer may be best served by a delayed payment to suit your cash flow, a large quantity in stock to cover surges in demand and a flexible returns policy to cover for break-ages. The seller may be interested in a premium price to move the produce upmarket, large production runs to reduce unit costs and a specification that reduces inspection costs.

Trading a higher unit price for delayed payment and a different specification for a flexible returns policy, and matching each other's needs for large production and order quantities, provides each of you with a non-zero-sum settlement. You both make gains without diminishing the other's gains.

Not negotiable

A pressure ploy. Stake out a non-negotiable area, refuse to budge, and force the other negotiator to accept your exclusion of issues from negotiation.

The problem comes if what you are excluding from the negotiation is the central issue that the other negotiator wishes to nego-tiate about.

Some issues are non-negotiable, and we prefer to resolve the dispute by other means (war, litigation). But excluding issues does not make them non-negotiable, otherwise negotiation would narrow the negotiable issues to the ones they felt strongest in, or the one they were least concerned about.

Nothing is agreed

Nothing is agreed until everything is agreed.

LISTENING to a proposition does not commit you to agreeing to it (do not interrupt). Asking QUESTIONS about a proposition does not signify you agree with it.

Assert regularly that agreement on one issue is not final and must await consideration of the whole package (see LINKING).

Objection

A defensive move, signalling INHIBITIONS about your PROPOSAL. Unanswered, objections fuel the inhibitions of the objector.

Do not interrupt well-worn objections with well-worn answers:

- Listen to the objection.
- Ask QUESTIONS for clarification.
- Show empathy ("Yes, I see what you are getting at"), not contempt ("Yes, it's true that some less informed people do worry about that").
- Address the objection with a full and frank exposition to eliminate their concerns.
- If their worries are founded on a misconception, gently correct it, and support with a review of the benefits. Ask positively if their anxieties have been satisfied.
- When the objection refers to something your service does not cover, avoid trying to BLUFF your way round it.
- Direct their attention to how what they are worried about compares with the benefits from the rest of your proposal. An objection answered is a step towards an AGREEMENT.

Objective

Quantified objectives are meaningful; non-quantifiable objectives are suspect.

If your objectives are vague – "a better deal", "happier employees" – quantify them by considering the steps needed to achieve them.

- What constitutes a better deal?
- What would make the employees happier?

Set a range rather than choosing a fixed number. A range gives you negotiating flexibility and forces you to consider alternative trade-offs (your nascent negotiating STRATEGY).

Off the record

One way out of a DEADLOCK is through an off-the-record discussion. The PRINCIPALS meet for a private discussion, out of earshot of their colleagues, and agree to settle. If using a "washroom" ADJOURNMENT, check the stalls first in case an unnoticed outraged colleague puts the private talks on the record.

Use off-record moves only with negotiators you know well and TRUST.

Offer

Can be tentative or specific but should always be conditional: "If you do such and such, then I will do so and so."

When making tentative offers be specific about what they must do for you and be vague about what you could do in return.

Being too specific reveals your hand, causing them to revise their EXPECTATIONS, maybe to your disadvantage. Non-specific offers are suitable for ADD-ONS.

BARGAINING offers are always conditional and specific. If they say "yes" to a specific offer, you have an AGREEMENT.

Offer they must refuse

An OFFER deliberately set to be rejected. Contractors overloaded with work BID high to avoid winning a contract when not bidding at all would antagonise the buyer and endanger future opportunities.

To be used when you wish to avoid:

- low-profit contracts;
- contracts below a minimum value;
- places where you do not want to go;
- people you prefer not to deal with.

Introduce unacceptable conditions or demands that are outside the other negotiator's limits. Or deliberately declare something to be NOT NEGOTIABLE that is vital to them.

Problem: Sometimes the "offer they must refuse" is accepted and you are left to get on with it.

Offset

Increasingly common and a restriction on free trade. No direct transfer takes place between the supply of goods and the offset activity.

Offsets are largely political counters to local lobbying against foreign suppliers.

An offset deal is meant to bring new work to the domestic economy, but it is often merely work that would be placed in the country anyway.

On taking it personally

Negotiators are human: they get upset. Occasionally even seasoned negotiators get extremely angry, make THREATS, raise their voices, shout, curse and remonstrate. Sometimes they walk out and protest at the other negotiator's behaviour.

Most negotiators slip into unprofessional involvement some of the time. In negotiating, do not take it personally or we will all be worse off.

One good turn

A powerful but underrated influencing technique in the form "one good turn deserves another". It depends on the principle of RECIPROCITY.

Returning personal favours (called GUANXI in China) is the key to building life-long business (and political) relationships in all cultures. So watch for an opportunity to return a proportionate good turn to anyone doing you one. Your relationships depend on it, and your negotiated outcomes depend on your relationships.

The corollary is "one bad turn deserves another". It is best to act considerately towards others and not to treat their INTERESTS negligently. Those you meet on the way up you may also meet on the way down.

One-offer-only

A procedure whereby suppliers get one chance to offer their best PRICE in competition with others.

It is best used for the regular purchase of standard products that are well specified. It can also be used occasionally for expensive mandatory services (audits, banking and legal services, pension fund management, insurance, and so on). Test the market by calling for tenders for your business in fixed periods of, say, 2–3 years.

If the specification is unambiguous, there is nothing but price to negotiate. If there is no collusion between sellers, you can be sure of a competitive price (almost always somebody is willing to DISCOUNT a price for business).

If the specification is complex, or the purchase is so separated in time as to be unusual, purchase by negotiation. Not being too sure about what you want could lead you to specify something that negotiation could improve upon.

One price, one package

A seller's defensive ploy. You can expect the other negotiators to push you either on the PRICE or on the package, or on both. To clinch the deal they "need" this or that extra, or demand them as ADD-ONS inclusive of your quoted price (see YES, BUT).

- Apply the principle "this package, this price; that package, that price"
- Flush out all the extras or changes that the buyer wants to your proposed package. This blocks off a "yes, but" approach.
- Price these as another package.
- TRADE off changes in the package against the change in the price.

Failing to price package changes undermines their value (free gifts are seldom appreciated), and you miss an opportunity to teach the buyer that you negotiate by trading, not by unilaterally conceding.

Precedents are promises for the future.

One-truck contracts

A risky way to do business. You undertake a transaction with a minimum of discussion about the contingencies that might arise. If these contingencies are expensive, there is a RISK of a liability claim.

Hiring a truck with a minimum of fuss has its advantages: "one truck, $150 a day rental". But trucks are used for a purpose, and in using a truck all kinds of possibilities emerge:

- Who pays for repairs while the vehicle is on hire?
- Who recovers it if it breaks down?
- Who pays for fuel?
- Is it replaced if it is stolen or breaks down?

■ Who is legally liable for its mechanical condition?
■ Is it warranted for the use to which it is to be put?

Profitable rental companies have pre-printed contracts with every imaginable contingency covered either in detail or through LIFEBOAT CLAUSES (which is why they are profitable). Consider the possible contingencies in your deals and negotiate for them to be covered.

One-way streets

Contracts become one-way streets when they are written to benefit one party only (usually the party that wrote the contract). Challenge them line-by-line; rewrite them to reverse the one-way street in your favour; and when the other party complains, suggest the contract is written to benefit both of you. Take care with one-way street clauses that give the other party, not you, the right to:

■ terminate for financial difficulties (appointment of creditors' committee, administrators, receivers and liquidators);
■ terminate for breaches of material clauses;
■ warranties and indemnities covering risks;
■ assign the AGREEMENT in whole or in part.

Remedies: Do not sign one-way street agreements under any circumstances. Require MUTUALITY in contract design as a sign of mutual respect and partnership.

Option

Protection against gazumping (see GAZUMP). When buying, offer the seller an option instead of a mere deposit. This "locks in" the seller to the transaction and protects you from gazumping.

Offer a cash consideration for the purchase of a legally binding option to buy the property by a given date for an agreed PRICE. If for any reason you fail to buy the property, the seller keeps your option money. When you exercise your option to buy, set the option money against the purchase price.

Will a seller accept an option to purchase agreement? That depends on its terms.

Sellers have an interest in raising the PRICE of the option; the higher it is the more determined the buyer will be to exercise the option. If the option price is acceptable to you as a seller, it doesn't matter if the buyer sells on the same property later at a higher price. It's like estate agents paying you for selling your property, which is better than paying them anything from 1% to 3%.

Or else

An ultimatum ploy. "Either you meet our demands, or else we call a strike."

Such ploys can provoke the very resistance they are trying to overcome. If they believe that your THREAT is empty, or can be ridden out, they might choose to take the "or else" consequences rather than give in. They might be angry and defiant enough to take the "or else" option even though you have overwhelming POWER.

Order-taking

A sign of a jaded salesforce. Sellers who merely meet customers to take their regular orders are missing opportunities to negotiate better orders. It might be cheaper for a company selling from a regular low-value list to use a telephone-sales operation.

Over-and-under ploy

The impossible response to the impossible demand. The other negotiator sometimes springs an impossible demand upon you: "Give me 5% for a three-day settlement DISCOUNT."

Spring back with an over-and-under: "If you agree to a 5% premium for late payment."

Packaging

Unwrapping and rewrapping PROPOSALS to make them mutually acceptable. By repackaging the contradictory or overlapping parts of competing proposals you move towards BARGAINING.

Packages address the INTERESTS and INHIBITIONS of each party. If they are keen on the money (interest) but are worried about getting paid (inhibition), repackage your proposal to meet these requirements without jeopardising your own.

- Can you repackage them in a different way?
- What are the shared interests in particular options?
- Can you TRADE movement on one option for movement on a less important option?
- What might you want in return for offering them what they want?

Padding

A negotiating margin. The padded PRICE gives sellers negotiating room. When the buyer expects some movement and you have no room to move, you could end up losing the business, or buying it at the expense of your profits.

Pad prices when:

- you anticipate last-minute demands;
- they do not have final AUTHORITY;
- you expect a competitive re-bid ploy;
- dealing with price-blind clients;
- you can avoid a COST BREAKDOWN;

- you have to wait for your money;
- a COUNTER-TRADE proposition is likely;
- whenever you can get away with it.

Partner

A partner shares your problems and the profits. Disputes between partners originate from differing PERCEPTIONS of how each fits into the future direction of the business. Breaking up a partnership is more complicated than a divorce, so it is better to negotiate terms before the partnership is formed (or wedding is solemnised – a pre-nuptial agreement) rather than when a break-up is imminent:

- on how the assets and liabilities will be shared in the event of a dissolution or divorce;
- on the rules for removing somebody from the partnership who is incompetent or otherwise no longer suitable.

You feel the need for a partner most when you need access to capital or contacts. But why give away things you will value later for things you value now, if the consequence is that you have to share everything (the worth of the business, plus its profits) long after your initial needs have been met? Can you offer a high return on the capital invested rather than a partnership? Pay the lender off, then everything you created remains yours.

Patents and licences

Products and services can be licensed. The licensor receives income for creating a product or service that the licensee exploits in a defined territory.

Consider the following when negotiating licences.

- What is the licensor granting to the licensee and for which territory?

- What is the licensee entitled to market or sell?
- Which specific patents, trademarks and know-how is the licensor licensing?
- How exclusive is the licence?
- Is the licensee allowed to sell outside the territory?
- Can the licensor also supply, independently of the licensee, into the licensee's territory?
- Are other licensees of the licensor permitted to sell or supply in the licensee's territory?
- If the licensee fails to meet market targets, or to supply known demands for the licensor's products or services, can the licensor supply direct, or contract with another licensee to do the same?
- How much does the licensee pay for the licence and when?
- Is the licence fee a royalty on GROSS or NET turnover?
- If net, how is this defined?
- How regular are the payments to be?
- What separate accounts should the licensee keep? How regularly may they be inspected? Who will audit them?
- How long should the AGREEMENT last?
- What notice is required to terminate the agreement?
- Under what conditions can premature TERMINATION occur (breach of contract, BREACH OF FIDUCIARY TRUST, FORCE MAJEURE, bankruptcy of licensee, merger or takeover by another company)?
- What must the licensee undertake to do when the licence is revoked for any reason? What restrictions on the licensee are imposed? What happens to current stocks or client services?
- What obligations are there on the licensee to preserve confidentiality both in and out of contract?
- What guarantee of quality must the licensee give in respect of the production or supply of the licensor's goods or services?
- What prohibitions or restrictions are to be imposed on the licensee for supplying similar goods or services?

- What training and support is the licensor to supply to the licensee, and who meets the costs?
- How are disputes between the licensor and the licensee to be resolved and which country's law applies?

Patience

More than a virtue, patience is imperative. TIME is the most expensive cost of negotiating. Patience reduces time pressures:

- If the negotiation is likely to be a long one arrange coverage of senior staff so that other work does not suffer.
- Rotate staff to reduce isolation and fatigue.
- Reduce your reliance on the outcome of the negotiation by competing for other work.
- If you desperately need the business from a long-haul negotiation, consider your BATNA.
- Sit it out, but send patient people to negotiate because the least patient concede faster.

Penalty cause

Assurance against failure to comply with promises. The penalty can be a fixed or an escalating sum. When pressing for penalty clauses assert that if they have confidence in their performance they have nothing to fear from them.

Resist penalties if the nature of the work creates unique uncertainties, such as:

- unforeseeable geological conditions;
- narrow weather windows;
- special safety hazards;
- political instabilities that threaten access and egress;
- difficult legal complications or jurisdictions;

- dependence on events outside your control (FORCE MAJEURE);
- uncertain technologies;
- untested designs;
- reliance on client's data;
- subjection to client's changeable specifications and managerial directions.

Your performance guarantees operate only if:

- spares, inputs and material meet your own specifications;
- everybody connected with the process is trained to your standards;
- the working environment is suitable for the process;
- you have the right to on-site inspection, to replace or repair, and to decide if any working practice is in violation of your WARRANTIES.

Insist that the penalty clock stops if delays are caused by the client's failure to meet obligations; it is restarted (at your confirmation) only when the client complies. This moves all consequential critical dates to new later dates, not just the dates of the immediately affected segment.

Penalty clauses are sometimes used to beat "unfair trading", dumping or illegal subsidy legislation rules. The supplier quotes a PRICE with a substantial delivery penalty and ensures or expects delivery to be delayed. The late delivery penalties come into force which reduces the actual price paid. You get a reputation for poor delivery, but you get the business.

Pendulum arbitration

An arbitrator must choose one or other negotiator's FINAL OFFER and not seek a compromise between them. A negotiator could be encouraged to refuse to settle because an arbitrator's decision is a compromise between the two final offers and improvement in the other negotiator's final offer is bound to result.

When, however, the arbitrator is using pendulum arbitration the negotiator must ensure that the final offer is not too extreme because the arbitrator is likely to choose the other negotiator's less extreme position. Adjusting the final pre-pendulum arbitration offer to make it attractive to the arbitrator also makes it more attractive to the other negotiator. When both negotiators do this they become more conciliatory, which improves their chances of finding a solution.

Perception

Seeing ourselves as nobody else does.

Other people's behaviour influences your perceptions and what you perceive confirms, or amends, your ASPIRATIONS. The other negotiator attempts to influence your perceptions in order to:

- restructure them in their favour;
- shake your faith in the viability of your current offer;
- increase the sense of inevitability of settling at their current offer.

You structure your opponent's perceptions by your apparent:

- willingness to DEADLOCK;
- indifference to settling quickly;
- confidence that you have options;
- resolve not to compromise;
- professional success;
- confidence in your current PROPOSAL;
- willingness to listen;
- reasonableness.

Use the following ploys:

- Weaken your opponents' confidence. Ask for the criteria,

method of calculation, statement of the "facts", and references to precedent or convention that support their case; then look for inconsistencies, alternative "facts", dubious ASSUMPTIONS, omissions and unwarranted conclusions.

▨ Deter a resort to COERCION. Assert your desire for a negotiated settlement to save costs to both sides. Adjourn to "cool off" and think through the consequences of not coming to an AGREEMENT. Show willingness to continue negotiations for "as long as it takes".

▨ Enhance the viability of your own proposals. Show confidence in your presentation, your grasp of details, your willingness to understand their needs and to consider options that bridge your differences, and your intention of coming to an agreement as soon as possible (although you are more than willing to wait, if need be).

Performance bond

Varying degrees of onerous burdens imposed by powerful buyers on desperate sellers. Originally, the performance bond protected the client from shoddy work.

A performance bond concentrates your efforts to deliver your promises. If you fail, the buyer cashes the bond in compensation.

The performance bond could be irrevocable and unconditional and the buyer in a foreign jurisdiction may have a right to cash it, as the fancy takes him. To agree to this is an act of reckless desperation, irrespective of the quality of your performance. To refuse to agree to a performance bond disqualifies you on the grounds that you have something to fear, so in desperate circumstances you agree.

Performance bonds shift the RISK from the buyer to the seller (if buying, demand one). The risk in some jurisdictions is transformed from being one of performance to being whether the buyer will invoke payment regardless of your performance. The POWER balance and the jurisdiction determine whether you agree to their terms.

Unscrupulous officials sometimes press for a bribe as an inducement for them not to present the bond for payment, or in certain regimes, the official cashes the bond anyway and pockets the money (check with the commercial attaché at your embassy).

Perry Mason ploy

Behaving like legal counsel and interrogating the party you are trying to negotiate an AGREEMENT with.

The ploy consists of asking a string of QUESTIONS, the answers to which at first are apparently innocuous. As they receive the answer "yes", they move in for the "gotcha" question.

The ploy is illegitimate. There is no connection between the lead-in questions and the ultimate question. If you answer their questions they pronounce you "guilty". Hence it is best not to answer their questions at all.

Counter: Ask: "What exactly are you getting at?"

Personal relationships

Never underestimate their value. Only trespass on them once. Do not rely on them.

While you seek to cultivate sound personal relationships based on demonstrated TRUST and reliability, you must recognise that other people's commitment to your INTERESTS, when the bullet slides into the breech, is fragile.

Commercial negotiators, diplomats and BARGAINING agents inevitably form relationships, if only from getting to know each other. These relationships are important, however tentative they may be, because negotiating with somebody you don't know is more difficult than negotiating with somebody you do know.

The basic principle of establishing a personal negotiating relationship is to assist them to achieve their OBJECTIVE within the boundaries of your own. In short, do not take undue advantage of their predicament.

Persuasion

The most common form of disclosure when you face a problem.

People whose INTERESTS are different from yours are not easily persuaded if the stakes are important to them. When they are not persuaded by your reasonable, logical and sensible statements, you are frustrated, you become annoyed, and you perceive wickedness in their inability to see your point of view. The result is an ARGUMENT.

You limit the likelihood of failure by:

- attempting to persuade them of simple, easy-to-agree points, rather than complex, controversial issues;
- emphasising your eagerness for reaching an AGREEMENT, not for forcing them to comply (that is, do not mix persuasion with threats);
- restricting yourself to a few robust arguments in favour of your position which stand up to scrutiny, rather than diluting them with spurious arguments that collapse as soon as the weakest is challenged;
- appealing to their self-interest rather than recognition of what you deserve.

Phases of negotiation

All negotiations have a common phased structure no matter what they are about, whom they are between, what is at stake, where

they occur, what the culture is, or what levels of technology dominate the economy.

These common phases are prepare, debate (explore), propose,
bargain.

Although the phases are distinct, they may follow in different
sequences. A formal written OFFER posted to another party opens
the negotiation with a bargain (an offer the other party can say
yes to and conclude an AGREEMENT). More likely is that questions
will be asked (exploration), prices will be challenged (debate) and
alternative suggestions made (PROPOSALS). It could be that the
receiver of the bargain will want to check the details, research the
options and consider their goals (PREPARATION).

The distinction between the phases is not in their sequence
(because there is no single correct sequence) but in the different
behaviours associated with each phase. The training proposition
is that by identifying the phase of the negotiation – and by avoiding behaviour that is less helpful to that phase and generating
behaviour that is more helpful – negotiators can improve their
effectiveness.

The extent to which negotiators are skilled in the behavioural
tasks of the negotiation for each phase will determine the quality
of the deals they achieve. Everybody is a phased negotiator,
whether they are aware or ignorant of the phases.

There are various phased models. The first to appear, in 1962,
was by Ann Douglas, whose background was in American labour
relations. It consisted of three phases: establish the negotiation
range; reconnoitre the range; and precipitate the decision-reaching
crisis. In 1972, the author of this book published an 8-step model
(prepare, argue, SIGNAL, propose, PACKAGE, BARGAIN, CLOSE,
agree), later simplified to FOUR PHASES. Philip Gulliver published
an 8-phase version in 1982 based on comparing American labour
negotiations with those in a low-tech African society. Five-, six-
and seven-step versions also exist.

All phased versions of negotiation behaviour have a common

source in observing what negotiators actually do rather than imagining what they ought to do.

Phoney deadline

A MANIPULATIVE PLOY used to pressurise the other party into a quick decision by creating a phoney deadline:

- If you do not decide now, the opportunity to buy will close.
- We have to reach AGREEMENT before the board meeting.
- This has to be settled before close of business today.

If you believe the DEADLINE is real, you might make a quick decision and regret it later. Deadlines are often arbitrary, unreal and phoney. Question them.

Positional bargaining

Build yourself a position and fortify it. Negotiators can get stuck in defending positions instead of seeking a solution within a range of options. Defending a position can lead to attacking the other party's position, which leads to destructive ARGUMENT and DEADLOCK.

Repetitive defences of positions harden the negotiator's stances and stifle creativity (see PRINCIPLES 2).

Positional posturing

Sometimes confused with POSITIONAL BARGAINING. Posturing by refusing to negotiate or move from a posture has nothing to do with BARGAINING. "If you want to go to the movies, it is *Quantum of Solace* or nothing", is coercive ultimatum posturing and not bargaining. Negotiation is the management of movement; posturing demands surrender of the other party. It sounds tough, it is aggressive and it treats the other party as a doormat. Not a recommended negotiation behaviour.

Power

Like the wind, felt rather than seen. You have power over the other negotiators to the extent that you can induce them to do something they would otherwise not do, or you can stop them doing something they otherwise would.

Your BARGAINING power, as is the other negotiator's, is a function of the relative costs of disagreement to each of you. Specifically:

$$\text{your bargaining power} = \frac{\text{disadvantages to them of rejecting your terms}}{\text{disadvantages to them of accepting your terms}}$$

$$\text{their bargaining power} = \frac{\text{disadvantages to you of rejecting their terms}}{\text{disadvantages to you of accepting their terms}}$$

In general, if your power ratio is greater than unity (the disadvantages of rejection are larger than the disadvantages of acceptance), then you may have bargaining power over the other side.

Operational content can be derived by calculating the disadvantages (not all of them numerical; some are qualitative, such as "loss of face" or "appearing weak") of rejecting their OFFER. These disadvantages must be probabilistic: there is no certainty that their last offer is their FINAL OFFER, or that the threatened, or implied, consequence (STRIKE, LOCKOUT, cancelled contract, divorce, war, damaged reputation, and so on) will materialise. Moreover, your estimates of the disadvantages of accepting their last offer may be pessimistic.

Power is subjective. It's in the mind. You perceive their power according to many influences on your mind, some of them unconscious, some mistaken and some manipulated by them.

Praising the product

Don't. It encourages suppliers to charge more.

Pre-emptive bid

An attempt to jump the queue before an AUCTION. You bid an amount sufficient to induce the owner to accept it in preference to waiting for the uncertain outcome of an auction. If the BID is "high" enough, the inducement is plain.

To apply extra pressure:

- make your pre-emptive bid conditional on its almost immediate, certainly early, acceptance;
- state that if the bid is rejected you will not re-bid subsequently at any PRICE whatsoever. Mean it.

Premium pricing

Premium products are marketed at higher PRICES than others. The price mark-up may not reflect anything substantial in terms of product differences. If the other negotiators perceive your product to be superior to substitutes, they might be persuaded to pay a premium price.

Preparation

The jewel in the crown of effective negotiation. Get this right and your performance in the negotiation dramatically improves.

The best preparation is knowing your business better than anybody else. If you do not know your business well enough, your rivals will teach you.

- What are my INTERESTS? (The reasons you are negotiating.)

- What are the issues? Itemise the details for negotiation.
- What do I want for each issue?
- How important is each want to me? Prioritise them using:
  - high importance (must get or definitely no deal);
  - medium importance (important to get or perhaps no deal);
  - low importance (like to get but will still deal).
- What are my entry OFFERS? Quantify them.
- What are my exit offers?
- What do I not want, and how badly? (See INHIBITIONS)
- What might the other negotiators want?
- What might be their entry offers?
- How far might they move?
- How might they prioritise their wants?
- What information have I got that helps me?
- What information could hinder me if disclosed?
- What information do I need to verify my ASSUMPTIONS?
- What is my STRATEGY? Keep it simple.
- What happens if it is not working? Select a FALL-BACK strategy.

Write everything down. A preparation planner is a useful tool for developing your ideas (see Figure 2). Your wants are listed in a column down the left-hand side of the paper.

- Allocate degrees of importance to your wants (high, medium, low) and collect them together in the column.
- Establish a range rather than a fixed number for each want.
- Write your entry offer for each want on the left and your exit offer on the right.

Price

First unassailable law of the MARKET: the selling price of something is not what it cost its owner, but what it is worth to the keenest person to acquire it.

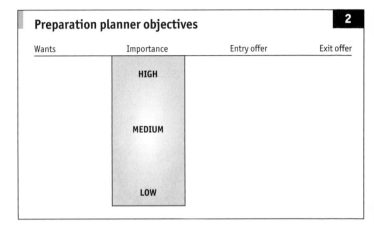

The total revenue from sales equals price per item times quantity sold. The total cost from producing the items equals cost per item times quantity produced. If total revenue minus total cost is greater than zero, you make a profit. If it is not, you do not. To stay in business, find enough buyers keen to acquire your output at a price that raises total revenue above total costs.

The trouble is that your costs are your affair but your selling price is set by the market.

Some people believe that all companies' problems boil down to price. To survive profitably, you must drive down costs per unit (search for efficiency) and find the price that captures the most profitable total revenue (net of marketing costs).

Troubles begin when companies kid themselves by versions of:

- altering attributions across cost headings;
- changing depreciation practice, and so on;
- "marginal cost pricing";
- pricing for "contribution to overheads";

- pricing to "fill unused capacity";
- pricing to "clear the unsaleable stock".

Price negotiation

PRICES are determined by MARKETS, but you do not sell to markets, you sell to people, and these people do not have perfect information. Imperfect information is both your edge and your torment.

If buyers are queuing six deep to buy your stock, your price will be higher than if you are in a six-deep queue of sellers waiting to sell it. But if it is down to price alone, consider getting out of that line of business.

A price negotiation is a ZERO-SUM game. Your most profitable strategies include the following:

- Widen the negotiation from price to other TRADABLES.
- Separate yourself from the competition.
- Form a queue with only one person in it: yourself.
- Go for the big numbers (test the quantity DISCOUNTS available from sellers; test the total revenue available from buyers).
- Go for the ADD-ONS.
- Test the buyer's price sensitivity.
- Test the seller's mark-up.
- Go for the co-operative relationship.
- Test the buyer's INTERESTS.
- Test the seller's reliability.
- Go for the mutual WIN-WIN (NON-ZERO SUM).
- Test the buyer's room for manoeuvre.
- Test the seller's room for manoeuvre.
- Enter not too close to your exit price.

Price versus cost

A ploy to protect a PRICE from a buyer's challenge. For example:

Seller: Do you want a low price or low cost?
Buyer: I don't follow you.
Seller: Low-priced products cost more when you use them. They break down more often and have a short life.
Buyer: You just want me to pay your high price.
Seller: Sure I want you to pay my price, but I also want you to benefit from a longer-lasting product with lower costs over its longer life than a cheapie.
Buyer: So?
Seller: Well, you pay my price only once, but how many times will you pay for the cheapie?

Price war

Avoid it. Move into some other business. Move upmarket or move downmarket or move sideways, but do not join in.

Price wars are won by the big battalions. If your market share is 1%, you will not drive a *Fortune* 500 competitor out of the market by slashing your prices. The competitor could give your 1% volume free to your customers and wait until you ran out of breath.

If you cannot keep out of a price war, the objective is to survive, not to win (for there are no winners).

Principal

The organ grinder. The advantages of dealing with principals are as follows:

- They make the final decision.
- They can authorise changes.

- They can accept unusual OFFERS.
- They are closest to the money.
- They can come to a decision quickly.
- You have equal status.
- You eliminate wallies.

The disadvantages of dealing with principals are as follows:

- There is no appeal against their final decision.
- They are not always on top of the details.
- They are too busy for slow-moving negotiations.
- They do not believe in equal status.
- They are emotionally involved with their properties.
- Some of them are wallies.

Principal–agent problem

The principal–agent relationship is fraught with potential conflict.

- An AGENT's fees (and expenses) reduce the money due to the PRINCIPAL (if selling) or add to the principal's costs (if buying).
- Agents may be more interested in clocking up their expenses than in completing the principal's transactions.
- Agents may misuse a principal's confidential information on the minimum acceptable deal and go for the deal that earns the quickest fee, not one that is best for the principal. They may also go for the deal earning them the biggest fee and not the one that is attainable (and still pocket their expenses).
- Busy agents may not give their full attention to your transaction because their other clients pay them higher fees.
- Agents (abroad) may work for the other side and take a fee from each party.
- Agents may be incompetent, indolent or corrupt.

Be careful of contract clauses that give the agent POWER to
bind you to what they agree with a third party without you con-
senting beforehand. They could lumber you with a poor deal
because they are desperate, going broke, dishonest, taking kick-
backs, incompetent, using your deal as a "special OFFER", in a
"sweetheart relationship" with the other party, or for nefarious
reasons known only to themselves.

Remedies: See AGENT.

Principled negotiation

Getting to Yes, by Roger Fisher and Bill Ury, promotes an approach
to negotiation far removed from the STREETWISE school of
manipulation. It recommends four guiding prescriptions:

- People: separate the people from the problem.
- INTERESTS: focus on interests, not positions.
- OPTIONS: generate options for mutual gain.
- Criteria: insist the outcome is based on objective criteria.

The four prescriptions are supported by people who see traditional negotiation as too competitive, too adversarial and too
subject to personal pressures, THREATS and intimidation.

1 People

Separating the people from the problem is something principled
negotiation shares with MEDIATION. Issues should be decided
without personal rancour on their merits and not influenced by
who is involved, positively or negatively. Sometimes, however, the
people are the problem.

2 Interests

Focusing on interests, not positions, is valid general advice. But
what principled negotiation considers to be POSITIONAL

BARGAINING is POSITIONAL POSTURING and not BARGAINING at all. Coercive demands are not negotiating. Insight into the important role of interests is of immense value to negotiators, as is the advice to avoid getting stuck on positions, unable to move at all. But downplaying the role of negotiable issues and positions is misleading. No negotiation can be concluded without detailed consideration of the issues, which inevitably means considering the merits or otherwise of the positions. Acquiring a product satisfies an interest, but what it costs, when it is delivered, how it is repaired and maintained, and what your rights are after the purchase are negotiable issues that deliver that interest. Concentrating only on your interests and neglecting the negotiable issues and positions is not advisable.

3 Options

Generating options for mutual gain is the most valid and unambiguous of the four prescriptions of principled negotiation. Adherence to a single solution to a negotiation problem is unnecessarily inflexible when more than one possible solution might produce an outcome acceptable to both parties. Fisher and Ury recommend a joint brainstorming session to tease out other solutions in a non-contentious atmosphere. The general rule for brainstorming is not to make judgments about any specific solution until the brainstorming session is over. The object of brainstorming is to identify as many practical solutions as possible in the TIME available.

4 Criteria

Insisting that the outcome is based on objective criteria is designed to select the appropriate solution from the several that may be on offer. Another way of putting this fourth prescription is to advise negotiators to submit to principle and not to pressure. Both versions appear reasonable because outcomes that are subjective are suspect and outcomes enforced by pressure (STRIKES, SANCTIONS, warfare or terrorism) are unfair (might is not necessarily right).

This does not make this prescription workable. Most negotiated solutions include objective data (how many days off, how cold is the temperature, how noisy is the airport) and may also include principles (last in, first out, poorest pay least, punish lawbreakers). But in every proposed solution lurks a principle, and one person's "objective" criteria may trump another person's "objective" criteria. Indeed, people choose their criteria to bolster the merits of their solution. Negotiators disputing solutions are usually disputing different criteria. This moves the dispute over solutions to a dispute over criteria and weakens the "reasonable" appearance of the fourth prescription.

Another connection between principled negotiation and mediation is the recommended resort to the assistance of a third party in a negotiation. Except for large-scale, usually government-backed, negotiations, third-party involvement is likely to prove expensive and unrealistic in most day-to-day negotiations, even if in theory such interventions might be useful.

Principles 1

Sometimes it is necessary to rise above them.

Negotiators who affirm to having principles often mean the beliefs that sanctify their prejudices. These people are extremely difficult to negotiate with, for their "principles" are a barrier to movement.

Principles 2

"Never yield to pressure, only to principle." (Roger Fisher and Bill Ury)

General principles that are independent of the negotiators are seen as aids to agreement. Instead of battling over conflicting demands, the negotiators search for objective criteria to judge the merits of alternative solutions.

If objective criteria are agreed (and this is not certain: see FORMULA BARGAINING), these become the principles that determine the joint solution.

You appeal to criteria independent of both of you:

- "fair standards" or "fairness" generally;
- market valuation;
- scientific measurement;
- legal precedent;
- actual costs;
- agreed objectives;
- equalisation of misery/profits/RISKS.

This does not avoid a dispute about the criteria. You may have to modify your demands in the light of the mutually chosen criteria, and you must be willing to do so.

If pressure is applied, insist on determining the issue by principles. If they have the POWER, however, it is usually decided their way, not yours. This is the weakness of this principled approach: there is seldom a unique set of agreed objective criteria for each dispute. Indeed, the parties can DEADLOCK over the choice of criteria, with each backing a selection that enhances its own position, taking them back to the problems of POSITIONAL BARGAINING.

Priorities

Best sorted out in PREPARATION, not while negotiating face-to-face.

Wants are not all weighted with the same degree of priority otherwise there would be little room for movement. Some issues are more important than others, and their ranking should be decided beforehand.

It is in the difference in priorities with which the negotiators approach the issues that the solution is found:

- Anything that the other negotiators value more than you is open to a TRADE for those things that you value more than them.
- It is not what it is worth to you that is decisive, it is the relative value to them.
- Your low priorities are not "giveaways"; they may value them more than you do.
- Paradoxically, the more they value particular outcomes the more POWER they give you if you value them less than they do.
- Power is balanced when the values of the issues to each of you are inversely related – what you value most is valued least by them; what they value most is valued least by you.

Events in the negotiation revise your priorities. Establishing your priorities is an organising not a stultifying activity. It ensures your grasp of the detail.

Prisoner's dilemma

There is no correct solution to a dilemma: that is why it is a dilemma.

You face many dilemmas in negotiating: where to open, when to move, whether to agree or DEADLOCK. You resolve these dilemmas by choosing, but your choice cannot be reversed.

Prisoner's dilemma is a mind game that illustrates the meaning of a dilemma. Two suspects are questioned by the district attorney (DA), who suspects them of having committed a major crime but does not have enough evidence to convict them. The DA does have enough evidence to convict them both of a lesser offence.

The prisoners are interviewed in separate rooms with no possibility of communication. They are each given a choice between confessing and not confessing to the serious crime. The DA's proposition is as follows:

- If you confess, but your partner does not, you turn state evidence and go free and your partner gets 20 years.
- If you both confess, you each get ten years.
- If neither of you confesses, you each get two years for the lesser offence.

If you were a prisoner, what would you do? Your consideration of the options and your hesitation over which to choose is an example of a dilemma.

Even if you trust your partner, he might depend on you not confessing and confess to get an early release (you get 20 years); or he might think exactly the same as you and confess, which gets you both ten years; or he might not confess and nor might you, so you both get two years. But whichever you choose, you are dependent on what your partner chooses.

Dilemmas are relevant to the negotiating situation. They help spell out the implications of the COMPETITIVE STYLE (doing what is best for yourself) and the CO-OPERATIVE STYLE (doing what is best for both of you). Going for short-term gains (whatever is best for you) can severely damage your long-term gains. Going for long-term gains (not exploiting your BARGAINING position) could be beneficial in the long run, but it is also risky in the short run if you are modifying your gains with someone who regards you as a one-off temporary PARTNER. (See TIT-FOR-TAT.)

Problem solving

Requires TRUST between the parties and confidence in each other's motives. Unilateral attempts to problem-solve a dispute expose you to STRATEGIC INTERACTION by the other negotiators if they continue to use a COMPETITIVE STYLE.

Problem solvers aim to:

- maximise joint gains;
- focus on common INTERESTS, not differences;

- be non-confrontational and non-judgmental;
- apply standards of "fairness", "common sense" and "reasonableness" (see PRINCIPLES 2).

They believe the other negotiators can be motivated to replace egoism with enlightened self-interest.

Procedure

Formal negotiating procedures are common in COLLECTIVE BARGAINING.

Procedure agreements between a TRADE UNION and an employer set out formal recognition of the rights and INTERESTS of each side.

Employees are usually required to take up any GRIEVANCE they have with their immediate manager. A FAILURE TO AGREE means the next level of management must be contacted, usually through, or accompanied by, an officially recognised shop steward.

If the shop stewards cannot settle the grievance, the local union official will be accorded higher-level access within the company. Where the company has more than one plant, the higher-level management will deal with the national officials of the union.

A grievance that survives the early opportunities for resolving it is usually of significance to both sides. The union will take a view on the significance of the members' grievance and how it relates to union policy. In theory, this filters out trivial grievances. In practice, the union removes the filter when it wishes to impose pressure on the company by letting grievances through to use up management TIME.

Companies negotiating formal procedures with a union should do the following:

- Reject closed shops or 100% union membership agreements.

- Require that union membership remain a voluntary decision of the employees.
- Insist that non-members will not be discriminated against in any respect (they will have a parallel grievance procedure).
- Require the AGREEMENT to be of fixed (renewable), rather than of indefinite, duration.
- Include a statement that "no accredited shop steward will be accorded special privileges as an employee and at all times will be subject to the normal disciplinary rules that apply to all employees".
- Reserve their absolute right to communicate directly with all employees on any matters and at no time concede this as an exclusive right of the union.
- Exercise this right on a regular basis, because communicating with employees only in crises with the union can be counter-productive.

Progress payment

Reduces exposure on long-lead-time projects. Paying for material for major construction projects imposes costs on the supplier (the capital tied up has a cost in its other profitable uses). There is also a RISK of financial failure by the client, of a change of government policy or a change of government, and of a cash crisis in your own operation.

Progress payments are made for identifiable progress in the project. They can be triggered by completion of specific stages (milestones), from the arrival of the materials for processing, through to delivery on site and to fabrication.

Other systems include the following:

- Paying up to one-third of the cost of signing the contract.
- Paying one-third at specified stages during the project.
- Paying one-third (less 5%) on completion.

■ 5% retained balance is held as a security against unforeseen, or hidden, failings in the structure and unwillingness on the supplier's part to rectify the problem.
Demand interest on the retained balance.

Promise

Best kept.

Proposal

The only thing that can be negotiated. You cannot negotiate an ARGUMENT, a belief, an opinion, a prejudice, a principle, a hope, a GRIEVANCE, a fancy, or a fact.

■ A proposal is a tentative solution.
■ A bargain is a specific conditional OFFER to settle.
■ Proposals are best made by putting the condition first – "if you will do the following, then I am prepared to consider doing such and such".
■ If they do not accept your conditions, they cannot enjoy the benefits of your offer.

A proposal discloses information about your settlement range, it being impossible to propose and simultaneously hide your offer. That is why your proposal is specific about what you want them to do, and vague about what you would do in return. The vagueness ("consider", "look at", and so on) loosens your commitment to a specific number or course of actions.

Some negotiations require (by statute, custom, necessity, convenience or tactical advantage) that initial proposals be made in writing. These should follow an entry offer format:

■ padded if open to informal negotiation (answering a request for broad details of charges);

■ less padded if open to formal negotiation (approaching an imminent decision or two-offers-only);

■ close to an exit offer if a competitive BID (ONE-OFFER-ONLY).

Verbal proposals have the advantage that you avoid the necessity of revealing your entry point before you have assessed their EXPECTATIONS through constructive debate. They have the disadvantage that you can fumble the presentation, disclose too much about your PRIORITIES and true ASPIRATIONS (see NON-VERBAL BEHAVIOUR), and make premature CONCESSION exchanges. To obviate these disadvantages, proposals should be:

■ stated briefly;
■ without long explanations;
■ summarised.

Avoid an instant response to a proposal (written or verbal). Seek:

■ clarification and understanding;
■ details of criteria used;
■ the thinking behind suggestions.

Do:

■ listen to the answers;
■ treat each item neutrally;
■ summarise your understanding;
■ look for bridges between your respective positions;
■ consider possibilities for PACKAGING.

Psychology of negotiation

The two great drives of human endeavour are our MOTIVATIONS and our cognitive PERCEPTIONS. These do not always match.

Motivations are best summed up by Maslow's hierarchy of needs, which he arranged in an ascending order of importance as each level of need is satisfied.

1   Physiological (hunger, thirst)
2   Safety and security
3   Love and belonging (acceptance)
4   Self-esteem
5   Self-actualisation
6   Knowledge and understanding
7   Aesthetic

Experimental and empirical evidence for Maslow's needs, particularly for the higher levels, is mixed. But as a working hypothesis they appear to fit most of the facts.

- **Physiological.** People who are starving are hardly likely to be concerned about status (unless it is related to access to food), but satisfy the basic needs and the other needs come into play. For negotiators, these needs are important.

- **Safety and security.** A buyer in a new MARKET chooses products that meet his or her security needs (well-known brands, not new ones that might be risky). This is why positioning your product as safe and secure pays off with new buyers entering the market.

- **Love and belonging.** Negotiators with a need to be loved (or respected) are vulnerable. They behave according to what they think is pleasing to whomsoever they are with. They try to please everybody. There is no pleasure in dealing with them. Either experience improves their performance, or they quit the business.

- **Esteem.** Self-esteem, such as the belief that we are worthy because of our professionalism, is a powerful motivator. In negotiating a good deal for our side, or by making the other side work hard for their gains, we become proud of our achievements, especially when set against recognised perceptions of the difficulties involved in achieving what we did. Self-esteem gives us confidence when we negotiate.

■ **Self-actualisation.** This comes from demonstrably achieving first-class results in negotiation, which stretched us to the limits of our powers. The appeal of a "search for excellence" message finds a response among managers driven by this motivator.

■ **Knowledge.** Our cognitive perceptions of the world – the set of beliefs that we work to – have roots that go deep into our psychology, our past, the past of the country we grew up in and our perceptions of the world as adults. International negotiations are particularly fraught, as the cognitive structures of the collective entity known as the nation are not easily or quickly changed. This explains why critics of their country's negotiating stances on certain international issues, who have not themselves sought or been elected to public office – and thereby have never had to compromise with the public's cognition of these issues – can often see rational "solutions" to these problems and are perplexed at the failure of the government to adopt them. However, in the circumstances, these rational solutions are impractical, in the sense that nobody articulating them could get elected.

■ **Aesthetic.** Our cognitive disposition includes our prejudices, folk myths and taboos. Negotiating with union representatives also involves negotiating with people imbued with a sense of the (often mythical) history of their union.

There is not always a common language accepted by the negotiators:

■ "Profit" to a manager may mean "exploitation" and "theft" to a union member.
■ "Efficiency" could be perceived as "slave driving".
■ A "good deal" to one negotiator could mean a "rip-off" to another.

Internationally, the paucity of common meanings separates

the negotiators of more than one country and political system. Consider the different interpretations of the words democracy, justice, rights, welfare, equality and defence found among member states of the UN.

There is always a temptation to find contradictions in the cognitive disposition of other negotiators. People are capable of holding passionately to totally contradictory attitudes and to having beliefs that are contradicted by their actions. These intrude into the negotiation as naturally as people blow their noses.

- Attacking somebody's belief system is never successful.
- If a negotiated peace requires the other side to suspend its entire belief system as a first step, there is little hope of success.

Hence consider how to advance your PROPOSALS without:

- setting off psychological resistance;
- antagonising or threatening the other negotiators' belief systems;
- undermining their personal motivations.

Instead:

- recognise the legitimacy of the other negotiator's personal motivations;
- refrain from disrespect towards their system of beliefs (no matter how weird you consider their beliefs to be).

Public stance

A COMMITMENT PLOY. By taking a public stance, the negotiator signals commitment to the declared outcome, ostensibly putting pressure on the other negotiators. It sometimes works. The other negotiators know that you cannot back off from a public statement without considerable loss of face. This induces them to believe that you intend to fight might and main for your publicly declared OBJECTIVE. In consequence, they give more than they intended.

Alternatively, your public stance imprisons your negotiating flexibility. A reasonable compromise is excluded because it threatens your public credibility.

Journalists are not given to explanations in public interest stories: either you won or you gave in. Your heroic "statesmanship", your finesse, your brilliantly executed manoeuvres are lost in the headline "Big Mouth Gives In".

Public stances complicate already complicated disputes. Neither side can move because it has publicly declared that it would not do so.

Agreement is inhibited by public stances. Think carefully before going public on a negotiating objective, especially in response to the other negotiator's public statements.

Questions

Important advice to all negotiators: ask questions and listen to the answers.

Open questions are better than closed ones. Examples of open questions include the following.

- How did you calculate the rental charge?
- What should I do about office security?
- What suggestions do you have for settling this compensation claim?

Open questions invite the listener to respond with extended statements rather than with yes or no answers.

Examples of closed questions include the following.

- Do you think this policy is fair?
- Are you in favour of an options clause?
- Can you redraw this boundary?

Closed questions are the most common questions, yet they are the least effective in securing information. There is not a lot you can do with a yes or no answer. The room for signalling is restricted, and even if the answer is clear – they say "no we do not want it" – you are not told anything about whether some adjustments in the PROPOSAL would satisfy them.

To unblock DEADLOCK, ask open questions. Consider the type of question you are about to ask. You want to get the most detailed and helpful answers that you can, so ask the right questions (content) the right way (open, not closed).

Question no-nos

Avoid questions that:

- expose you to mockery;
- expose your ignorance;
- are sarcastic in tone;
- are embarrassing;
- cause trouble;
- are point scoring.

Question proposal

Less assertive than a PROPOSAL statement. It is usually in the form: "If I agree to X, will you agree to Y?", inviting a negative response and suggesting you are unsure of what you want. Restyle as: "If you agree to Y, then I could consider agreeing to X".

Question the criteria

A ploy to undermine the other negotiators' PROPOSAL. Proposals that are based on facts, rules, formulae, ASSUMPTIONS, precedents and interpretations of "fairness" are vulnerable to how they have been formulated.

- Ask them to explain how they arrived at their proposal.
- What data did they use to calculate their figures?
- What statement of principle has formed the basis of their claim?

Watch out for references to:

- "normal" assessments;
- "standard practice";
- "straightforward" yields;
- "present values";

- "common knowledge".

These could hide phoney assumptions not applicable in your case.

Compelling the other negotiators to justify their proposal and its derivation enables you to:

- quibble with their assumptions;
- challenge facts;
- learn something about a MARKET with which you are unfamiliar;
- decide on the relevance of their criteria;
- query the reliability of their sources;
- check on the accuracy of their arithmetic;
- question the valuation of intangibles.

Exploring criteria creates negotiating opportunities that were hidden in the plausibility of jargon or assumed expertise.

If you disagree with the criteria the other negotiators have used, you have a more defensible negotiating position than if you accept the criteria but disagree with the conclusions.

Quick deal

Often regretted.

Quivering quill

A buyer's pressure ploy. Negotiators close to an AGREEMENT experience euphoria. The seller is feeling pleased at the prospect of earning the value of the deal, perhaps with some of it as a COMMISSION.

The buyer's pen hovers over the contract. The seller's anxieties leap upwards: "What do you mean you need another 2% off the PRICE?"

The buyer puts the pen down and sits back. Panic in the seller: "Look, if I give you 1% will you sign now?"

The buyer picks up the pen and leans over the contract. The quivering quill having quivered, quivers on. "Make it 1.5% and we have a deal?" Desperation in the seller: "Okay, okay, just sign it."

Counter: Same as for YES, BUT. Control your euphoria until the deal is signed (see PATIENCE).

Rapport

Helpful, but not sufficient to secure a negotiated AGREEMENT. Lack of rapport inhibits agreement.

You can help establish rapport by:

- matching your pace to the other negotiators' (particularly across cultures);
- taking a genuine interest in their contribution;
- steering gently towards the settlement you are looking for.

Realistic offer

An OFFER that can be defended credibly, not one that is fanciful. An offer's credibility is decided by the other negotiators.

- If the other negotiators believe your offer is realistic, then it is realistic.
- Unrealistic offers cause dissent and the other negotiators could break off.
- The further apart you are, the longer it will take to negotiate a solution.
- The other negotiators may be shocked by your offer, but might accept your explanation and adjust their own EXPECTATIONS.

Reciprocity

A universal principle found in all cultures. If people aid, assist or do you a good turn or any favour, they may do so for the purest of motives. However, should an opportunity arise for you to do them similar favours and for some reason you fail to reciprocate, you risk causing deep offence, even to those (saints excluded) who helped you without thought of creating an obligation on your part. The principle of reciprocity lies deep in the human psyche (and is familiar to our nearest relative, the chimpanzee).

Reciprocity links what others do for you to what you will do for them – "you scratch my back and I'll scratch yours". The reciprocity exchange is implicit, whereas the BARGAINING exchange is explicit. Reciprocity is an unenforceable implicit obligation. Withdrawing future favours and terminating the relationship punishes non-reciprocation. Negotiators, carelessly ignoring their reciprocal obligations, do themselves no favours.

Rent

Rentability determines property values. It is what the asset can earn in the MARKET.

If negotiating for the landlord, maximise the net lettable space; if for the tenant, minimise it. The net lettable space is what is usable by the tenant (whether they use it or not). Watch for:

- measurements running from inside the window alcove to the wall not the skirting board;
- deductions for central heating apparatus by the walls (when letting, fix a wooden shelf over them and count the space back in);
- how columns in the floor area are treated (if leasing check that the space they occupy is excluded);
- how stairs, landings and lifts are calculated;

- charges for common toilets;
- anywhere showing evidence of use – for example, cabinets in the common areas.

Rent review

Rent reviews adjust RENTS to MARKET conditions.

The PRICE per square unit of lettable space is determined by what somebody is willing to pay for it. Be guided by the rents realised in adjacent or similar buildings.

Most rents are for fixed terms which do not coincide with market movements in supply and demand.

The LEASE will include a provision for a rent review at specified dates.

- If you are a landlord in a tightening market, impose an "upward only" rent review.
- If you are a tenant in a slackening market, delete "upward only".
- Landlords should regularly inspect the property to check for chargeable use and to spot misuse.
- Tenants should require notice of an inspection to remove evidence of use of uncharged space.
- Tenants should research the market for going rates for lettable space.
- Tenants should check the earlier measurements of the property in case some structural change has occurred and its rentable implications have been overlooked.
- If facing increased rents, tenants should list the defects to TRADE increased rent for repairs.
- Landlords can avoid this by imposing full repair and insurance (FRI) terms in the lease, preferably on both an external and internal basis.

Landlords face costs in finding new tenants; tenants face costs in finding new premises. These costs are avoided by negotiating a new AGREEMENT, but they are willingly faced if the offered terms are onerous.

Changes in circumstances are reasons for holding rents, so keep the landlord's letting brochures on file and re-read them before a rent review.

Reputation

Lose it and you reduce your opportunities. As your reputation depends on the PERCEPTION of other negotiators and not on your own, it is easily lost or damaged, sometimes without good cause. What reputation do you want? And with whom?

Establish a negotiating reputation: "This company must establish that it says what it means and means what it says, even if in the short run it costs more than it's worth."

A reputation, once undermined, is less easily put right: it takes only one dispute, where the balance of power is reversed, for a "tough" reputation to crumble in a single retreat.

Interpretation of motives is not an exact science, and the same action is judged differently by different negotiators. Being untrustworthy or dishonest damages a reputation, perhaps beyond repair. Deals bypass you, because of your reputation.

Resistance price

The exit OFFER where you prefer "no deal" to a deal on worse terms.

At what PRICE does it become unprofitable to do business? Do not confuse a desirable with a truthful bottom line. You do not know the full facts before you negotiate and circumstances may suggest your original resistance point is unobtainable, but make sure that you are not rationalising your surrender under pressure.

Your resistance price may be established arbitrarily by your seniors; beyond this point you get sacked. If it is unrealistic, the time to discuss this is during PREPARATION and not in a post mortem. Think through the implications of and the criteria used to determine your resistance price.

Restrictive covenant

A buyer's protective device. Buyers of businesses protect themselves from future competition by negotiating a restrictive covenant on ex-owners. The ex-owner is prevented from opening a similar business close to the original business. How close is negotiable.

For small businesses, the restrictive covenant bars them from trading within the locality; for national businesses the restriction may apply to the entire country, or even the world as a whole (although courts have ruled against this).

- The ex-owner may be barred from trading in that business, or one closely related to it, for a fixed term of years.
- The restriction may be confined to the current clients of the business and may permit the ex-owner to generate new business.
- The scope may be narrowly defined (brewing but not barring distribution of beer) or widely defined (design, manufacture, distribution and finance of the product).

Publishers impose highly restrictive covenants on authors which prevent them producing similar works for other publishers that "materially affect the sales of the book", even though they seldom agree not to publish similar books by other authors.

- Some restrictive covenants aim to protect proprietary information, particularly from their research and development personnel.

■ Licensors also impose similar conditions on the employees of licensee firms and require the licensee to guarantee protection of the licensor's know-how.

If asked to sign a restrictive covenant, a minimum STRATEGY would be to limit the extent and scope of the restriction and its duration.

Reversion

A useful clause to protect your INTERESTS in case of default or some failure to meet the contractual obligations by the other negotiators.

Insist that failure to meet obligations, or circumstances such as their bankruptcy (better still, their going into ADMINISTRATION), trigger reversion to you of all your rights, property and monies, irrespective of their obligations to others. This is particularly important in a licence AGREEMENT. Liquidators try to take over property as forfeit in a bankruptcy.

■ Make sure that your property unambiguously passes back to you.
■ Give notice of reversion immediately you discover failure on the licensee's part to meet the agreed obligations.
■ Insert in the agreement that your notice of reversion is unconditionally sufficient for reversion to take effect.

Review

Post-negotiation review of both successful and unsuccessful negotiations is essential to long-term success. Like PREPARATION, the review should be structured. Use the original preparation plan as the basis for evaluating performance.

■ How does the negotiated outcome compare with your intentions?

- How did the process unfold?
- What events were unexpected?
- Where in the process do you think you did better/worse than you expected?
- What were the main mistakes?
- What were the successes?
- What was the most important lesson of the negotiation?

Draw up a list of actions to transform these lessons into improvements in future performance.

Risk

Never eliminated, but it can be reduced or priced. Risk is the companion of TRUST. Reduce risk as follows.

- Seek collateral.
- Restrict their discretion.
- Seek guarantees.
- Require a performance bond.
- Insist on a deposit.
- Sell or buy forward.
- Help them count the money.
- Help them collect it.
- Factor your invoices.
- Sell or take an OPTION.
- Insist on regular payments.
- Find out what the trouble is and what will put it right.
- Spread the risk across more than one basket (if you cannot watch the basket).
- Calculate income conservatively and costs liberally.
- Cut your losses.
- Charge more for the risk.
- Judge worth by expected value (see DECISION ANALYSIS).
- Propose a contingency deal.

Royalties

Authors get royalties, but few live like royalty. Royalties are a percentage share in the retail price of the work, ordinarily about 10% for hardcover books and 7.5% for paperbacks, and then escalating moderately as sales increase.

Authors should follow these guidelines.

- Require that royalties escalate quickly and the qualifying quantities are reduced.
- Watch for the "new edition" ploy, that is, the royalty clock restarts with each new edition. Go for a continuous count.
- Challenge their estimates of resetting costs, especially if you have supplied the text on disk.
- Never sell your work for a fixed sum; poor royalties are better than none.

Rules

In negotiation there are none.

What is proper is decided by the negotiators involved, and even they have no right of "appeal".

Informal "rules" have emerged, but they have no status other then what you accord them. For every rule there is an exception and for every negotiator there is a time and circumstance where the rule is abandoned.

Some so-called rules of thumb might include the following:

- AGREEMENTS should be honoured.
- SANCTIONS are permissible as complements to the negotiation but not as substitutes.
- Solutions should not be imposed on a take-it-or-leave-it basis.
- Neither negotiator should interfere in the internal affairs of the other to disrupt their negotiating position or cohesion.
- Negotiators should act in "good faith" (*ex bona fide negotiari*) and not behave in a reprehensible and destructive manner.

All these rules, and many others, are breachable. Often one negotiator abides by one interpretation of a rule and the other by another.

- The alleged dishonouring of an agreement is the subject of many renegotiations.
- At what point a sanction is unacceptable as a negotiating ploy is hotly contested by negotiators.
- Sometimes take-it-or-leave-it is all that is left when faced with obstinacy.
- Negotiators interfere in each other's affairs – that is what propaganda, public stances, leaks, rumours and THREATS are all about – to weaken the opposing coalition.
- Courts and ARBITRATION sittings are full of disputes about good faith.

Russian front

A ploy to make you accept one unpalatable OPTION by forcing you to choose between two unpalatable options, with one of them so unpalatable that you opt for the lesser one.

It is an allusion, from "B" movies, to the effect on soldiers of threats of being sent to the "Russian front" in the second world war. If the officer had the POWER to send someone to the Russian front, he could exact compliance with his wishes. The soldier cringed: "No, no, anything but the Russian front."

For example:

Q: "Either you send me a list of the ten least efficient people to be made redundant in your operation, or I will assume that it doesn't matter who is made redundant (including yourself) and I will sack ten people at random."
A: "Do you want the list typed or can I name them now?"

Salami

"A slice of cut sausage will not be missed." And it isn't. Can you salami your conditional PROPOSAL?

Children salami. You tell them not to go out of your sight in the park. They move away but stay in sight. Then they sit on the ground and you have to strain your neck to see them. Then they lie down so you have to get up to see them. They slide down the slope out of sight, but return every few minutes in case you are checking on them. Sometimes you see them, sometimes you don't, but they return enough times to stop you worrying too much, and anyway, you are getting tired jumping up and down to look for them. Then they go off for longer spells. You fret. They are off for an adventure but come back, eventually. They've salamied you.

Sanction

Any measure aimed to coerce the other party. Sanctions include the following:

Employee relations

- Go-slows.
- Overtime bans.
- STRIKES.
- Working to rule.
- Discriminating against identifiable groups.
- Work-time meetings.
- Refusing duty.

- Withholding necessary consents, documents, formal requirements.
- Occupying places of work to prevent others working.
- Picketing.
- Banning specified inputs.
- Refusing to work "blacked" (or scab) materials.
- Imposing bans of any kind.
- Rigorously applying safety rules.
- Mislaying materials, papers, information.
- Sabotage.
- Withdrawing special cover (safety, security).
- Sympathetic actions of any kind in support of other unrelated disputes.
- Clogging up the disputes procedures with spurious cases.
- Clogging up working procedures with health and safety enquiries.
- Prolonging meetings to waste TIME.
- Refusing to meet.
- Making public statements on confidential matters.

Commercial relations

- Cancelling contracts.
- Returning work unfinished.
- Holding on to drawings.
- Litigation.
- Calling in loans.
- Changing suppliers.
- Withholding consents.
- Mislaying necessary documents.
- Returning work on trivial technical grounds.
- Refusing to pay invoices.
- Holding up payments on one contract while there is a dispute on another contract.
- Refusing to maintain equipment.

- Withdrawing supplies except on onerous pre-paid cash terms.
- Calling a creditors' meeting.
- Appointing a receiver.
- Reporting alleged offences to an official agency, professional body or the general public.
- Withdrawing financial support.
- Liquidating the business.
- Selling shares.
- Placing votes in shareholders' meeting.
- Not electing directors, sacking employees (including directors).

Trade relations

- Discriminatory trade practices.
- Quotas.
- Tariffs and non-tariff burdens.
- Selective import controls.
- Withholding export guarantees.
- Restricting or banning investment.
- Selective and general trade sanctions.
- Dumping and accusing a country of dumping.
- Using vetoes in international organisations.
- Administrative delays.
- Embargoes.

International relations

- Withholding public support.
- Working behind the scenes to withhold support.
- Making public condemnations.
- Joining in coalitions to oppose specific INTERESTS.
- Freezing another country's financial assets.
- Imposing trade sanctions.
- Blockades.
- Using military force at any level, including war.

- Taking hostages.
- Taking punitive action against specific foreign citizens.
- Terrorism.

Secondary boycott

A coercive measure used by unions, presently illegal in the United States and the UK. Sympathy STRIKES in unrelated businesses to put pressure on an employer in dispute with its employees.

Secondary boycotts can be initiated by manufacturing a dispute (for example, health and safety) with your own employer that indirectly supports the employees in dispute with their employer.

Seeking clarification

PROPOSALS are not always clearly stated. Clarification is essential if you are unclear and bridge-building even if you are. People like to be treated seriously. Asking clarification QUESTIONS helps to build rapport. For example:

- Could you go over the second clause? I am not sure how you intend it to operate.
- Am I right in thinking that your liability clause would cover us up to two years from installation?

Questions sometimes finesse explanations that provide additional information about their wants and PRIORITIES. They can lead on to criteria questions.

Sell and lease back

A way to raise capital on your assets.

Lenders supply funds against first-class assets, such as prime site properties. You receive the capital for other purposes and lease back the properties you formerly owned and occupy. Sometimes there are tax regimes that are favourable to such deals.

This could be attractive to a takeover bidder who wants to release funds from the acquired company to reduce borrowings without damaging the income-earning capacity of the business. In the short term, the target for the takeover pays for your taking it over. The disadvantages are that you lose control of your properties, you may face rising RENTS at any subsequent RENT REVIEW, and your asset value is reduced.

Alternatively, you could place the company's properties into a separate subsidiary property company, which then borrows against its property and pays off the borrowings out of rents it charges the main company for use of the properties. The LOAN is secured against the property's assets and CASH is released for other purposes. When the mortgages are repaid the company still owns its properties.

Sell cheap, get famous

A buyer's ploy. Anybody new to a business has no track record. Newcomers cannot attract the premiums that go with experience. Buyers exploit this opportunity. The ploy persuades newcomers to accept a lower PRICE for their services.

Buyer: How many plants of this type have you designed?
Newcomer: This is my first contract.
Buyer: How many times have you been consulted about this type of business problem?
Newcomer: I did something similar in my MBA course.

The buyer has softened you up for a low-fee pitch. But he does not just push you down on price, he makes out he is doing you a favour:

- Design this plant for the fee I have suggested and you will establish your reputation and earn big fees on all subsequent work.
- Invest in solving this problem and you will soon be quoting with the big league consultants.

You sell yourself cheap to recoup the situation in future business. Some people, finding it hard to get started, offer their services free to clients just to get a track record

Counter: With difficulty, if your track record is a blank sheet of paper. If forced to accept a lower opening fee (do not fall for the "get famous" bit), go for a version of the contingency ADD-ON:

- If the design is accepted, then you pay me a second fee of 30%.
- If my solution is adopted, then you pay me another $15,000.

Sham offer

Using an entry OFFER to disguise your TARGET. You open with a sham offer of $400, leaving room to TRADE back to your target price of $380. Your exit price is $360. Opening at your target forces you to trade below it, which mocks your concept of a target.

If they accept your sham offer, apply the ADD-ON.

Shock opening

An abrasive pressure ploy.

The other negotiators open with a PRICE that is wildly outside your EXPECTATIONS. You are shocked into stunned surprise. If they follow through with a credible reason for their PROPOSAL you have to review your expectations.

The essential requirement for a shock opening is credibility. The other negotiators, hearing a shock opening, are forced to reconsider the basis of their own position: "Perhaps our price is too high?"

Even if the shock opening moves the other negotiators only part of the way from their expectations towards yours, your opening shock has been effective. There is a RISK, however, that you are so far away from their expectations that they break off the negotiations.

Shut up

Silence: there is not a lot of it about. Add to what there is by LIS-TENING more than you talk. Why? Because you know what is in your mind but you do not know what is in theirs. You will not find out by talking.

Shut up immediately after you:

- make a PROPOSAL;
- summarise;
- ask a QUESTION;
- reach an AGREEMENT (further talk can talk them out of the agreement they've just made).

Wait until they respond before you speak again.

Shut up when you have nothing to say. You do not have to fill every silence with words. Let the power of silence put pressure on them.

Signal

A subtle change in a negotiator's language, indicating a willingness to consider movement.

- What is "impossible" becomes "difficult".
- What was "never done" becomes "not normally done".
- What was "contrary to company policy" becomes "without precedent or prejudice".
- What was "no way" becomes "not under current circumstances".

Without signals, negotiators would have considerable difficulty in moving without giving the impression that they were about to surrender. Everybody signals – most people do not realise that they are signalling – but many negotiators miss signals because they are not LISTENING.

Some negotiators punish the signaller: "I see, so you're no longer holding your ludicrous opening OFFER?" This drives them back to ARGUMENT and delays a settlement. Do not rubbish a signal. Question it for clarification, encourage the other negotiator to elaborate:

■ You say you have a difficulty with my request. Is there any way that I could make it easier for you to meet my needs?
■ Under what conditions would your company be willing to make an *ex gratia* payment in circumstances like mine?

Signals are normally a prelude to a PROPOSAL, and no negotiation can get very far without proposals.

Sizzle

"Do not sell the steak, sell the sizzle." The world's most successful selling technique, developed by Elmer Wheeler, who believed that "the heart is closer to the pocket book that is the brain".

Find the sizzle in a proposition and put it to them. It goes down better than dry facts. It breaks through their INHIBITIONS.

In a competitive MARKET, why should an exporter ship with you rather than anybody else? Give a reason: "We do not sell cargo space (all your competitors have space), we sell guaranteed delivery."

Why should a bank choose your firm to liquidate a business? "We do not sell accountancy knowledge (our competitors are knowledgeable too), we sell hassle-free liquidation."

Counter: When buying, "buy the steak, not the sizzle".

Skimmer

Skimmers get between you and the deal and insist on being "taken care of" before the deal progresses much further. In some countries they pop out of the woodwork unexpectedly. They wait until the contractor is chosen and then get between the contractor and the client. That way they get paid off, no matter which of you wins the contract. Their position (perhaps a connection with the ruling family, perhaps a crucial role in the final decision) guarantees their ability to frustrate the deal. You pay up, or get nowhere. (See also GET-BETWEEN.)

Sometimes you can block skimmers by making a fuss with their boss, though the skimmer could be working for the boss, who prefers not to sully his reputation with an open demand for a bribe.

Try PADDING the PRICE with the skimmer's pay-off if the approach is made before you get to price. If the price is set – that is why you got the contract – the skimmer's large fee comes out of your profit.

Beware of people who claim to be able to block your deal but who are in fact only charming chancers. Pay them and you cut your profits, and if the real skimmers turn up, demanding their share of the cake, you are going to be working for nothing.

Skimming

A pricing STRATEGY. Some people are PRICE-blind when it comes to new products. They want the very best and expect to pay for it (if you don't go in high, they think your product is a cheapie).

Luxury cars, yachts, electronic gadgets and new products of all kinds are ripe for a price-skimming strategy. The MARKET is limited, deliberately so, but it is lucrative until the competition starts up (they see your pricey products and the people with money wanting to buy them).

Skim the "cream" with the high-price strategy, then expand output and lower prices gradually, as you work your way into the next segment of customers who want the product but are more price-sensitive than the people at the top end.

Skinner's pigeon

B.F Skinner (1904–99), a professor at Harvard University, claimed that human beings could be conditioned into behaviour patterns given the right stimulus and reward system. He demonstrated his theory by training a pigeon to pick out the ace of spades from a deck of cards, no matter how they were shuffled.

The lesson for negotiators is to consider the relative size of the brains of a pigeon and a human negotiator (roughly a pea to a cabbage). If a pigeon can learn to choose the ace of spades, how much cleverer is a human being learning from the behaviour of another negotiator?

Negotiators learn to say no if they find they get CONCESSIONS when they do so, hence do not stimulate their resistance by rewarding it.

Softness

Soft negotiators are characterised by their willingness to move in large steps from any position they adopt. Their basic fear is that of not securing an AGREEMENT. They:

- almost prefer any agreement to DEADLOCK;
- negotiate with themselves;
- crumble under threats;
- have an extensive repertoire for rationalising acceptance of any agreement offered;
- often talk too much;
- qualify any (often unconditional) OFFER they make with a

SIGNAL of how far they are prepared to move if it is not acceptable.

Split the difference

A settlement ploy. Negotiators stuck on two numbers can move to a settlement by "splitting the difference". You offer $80, they offer $40; splitting the difference gives you $60.

It sounds fair and equitable and sometimes it is. It can also be expensive; perhaps you cannot afford to split the difference.

To avoid this ploy, stick to numbers that do not have an obvious split point. If your offer is $83.5 and theirs is $40, it is not obvious what number splits the difference, and that which is not obvious is not as "fair" as that which is.

An offer to split the difference is risky because you disclose a willingness to move 50% of the difference between you. The other negotiators could exploit your SIGNAL and refuse to move, leaving you with a more difficult task in defence of your original number. They could also offer a different split: "I cannot go 50:50 but I will consider 30:70."

When an obvious split point emerges – you have proposed 10% and they have replied with 8% – move to bury the obvious split point by offering 9.85% (conditionally).

If the difference is trivial, there are bigger issues at stake and your relationship with the other negotiators justifies it, agree to split the difference as part of a larger package but not in isolation.

Standard terms

An alibi for loading the contract terms against you.

Sellers often print their terms and conditions on the reverse of their official letters confirming an order, or they are printed on the order forms that they expect you to sign. These standard terms always restrict their liabilities and are onerous to you, not to them, which is why they are printed.

Read them carefully. If you cannot accept them all, acknowledge their order in writing with a reference that it is accepted subject to your terms (enclosed), or to the exclusion of their specific term (reference number only). They may be so desperate to receive your goods that they waive their own terms. Later they could change their minds, but they are unable to enforce them once waived.

Printed terms are intimidating. They imply that they cannot be changed (which is why they are often printed close together, so that changes are near impossible). To avoid signing an official order form with its specific terms, send them an order in writing with your terms on it. Standard terms are negotiable, but only if you take the trouble to query them.

Strategic interaction

Jargon from GAME THEORY which describes how negotiators manipulate the information they pass to each other.

You do not know what is going on in the heads of the other negotiators. They are less than candid about their predicament because you might exploit this information. They think about how you are likely to react to their behaviour knowing that this is a reaction to your behaviour; how you think they think you think they think you think … Taken too far, concern with strategic interaction paralyses the negotiators into infinite regresses.

Strategy

Best kept simple. Complicated strategies fail within a few moves because the other negotiators have not read your script. They have a different plan.

The strategy is dependent on the circumstances and the issues in the negotiation. Not mentioning money, for example, might be a strategic objective when the value of what is for sale is not obvious (neither negotiator knows for certain the other negotiator's valuation). By keeping money in the background until they have ascertained enough information to set the "PRICE", the negotiators prevent an early "over" or "under" price being established.

Strategy should be flexible. If it is not working, do not persist. It should also be linked to your marketing and pricing plans.

But above all, remember what Robert Burns said about the "best laid plans of mice and men".

Streetwise negotiation

A popular approach to negotiation behaviour, associated largely with Chester KARRASS, author of *Give and Take: The Complete Guide to Negotiating Strategy and Tactics*. It appeals to people who want to know what works at the table and why, and what to do to defend themselves.

The streetwise concentrate on the use of popular MANIPULATIVE PLOYS and their counters from the real world of negotiation. This is ethically ambiguous: are you learning about these ploys to use them against others, or to protect yourself against their use against you? Negotiation is seen by the streetwise as a gladiatorial contest, in which the manipulative win and the softies go to the wall (unless they become streetwise first).

The three most popular ploys from Karrass (he mentions over 200 in his book) are the BOGEY, the KRUNCH and the NIBBLE, and his most famous strategy is to AIM HIGH. The main problem is that ploymakers require a constant supply of victims. If they run out of negotiating partners because their reputations precede them and their streetwise predilections have been found out for what they are, this makes them street dumb.

Stress

Negotiating is a stressful activity. You are:

- anxious about the outcome;
- emotional about their behaviour;
- unsure of the implications of offers;
- worried about the other party's intentions;
- concerned about not doing as well as you, or your peers, expect.

Stress cannot be eliminated, but it can be reduced. The professional negotiator tries:

- not to take things personally;
- to separate the merits of the issues from opinions of the personalities;
- to concentrate on their INTERESTS rather than on the numbers.

Basically, you should slow down the pace (ask more QUESTIONS), relax before and after sessions, and set realistic rather than fanciful targets.

Strike

Withdrawing labour is a legal right of employees.

Strikes aim to influence negotiation. The strike can be a prelude to a negotiated settlement or a substitute for one. Strikes over highly contentious issues are bitterly fought.

The strategy of the strikers is to prevent normal business being conducted. The strategy of the employer is to ensure that normal, or near normal, business continues.

If the strikers succeed in stopping normal business, it is a matter of resource attrition: which side runs out of resources first? If the company succeeds in continuing with normal business it is a matter of TIME pressure: how long before the strikers give up?

Public relations are important in strikes.

- Denouncing strikers as "extremists" when they manifestly are not is counter-productive.
- People who strike before exhausting the opportunities for negotiation are in a weaker position than those who are driven to strike by the intransigence of employers.
- Avoid being provoked or rushing into a strike; you might not be as indispensable as you think.
- Companies which make public statements about the "damage" done by, or the cost of, the strike strengthen the strikers (they feel they are achieving something).
- Strikes that appear likely to last a long time are over more quickly than those that appear to be short-term (hence, if asked how long you can take the strike, answer: "indefinitely").

Handling "peace" talks is difficult. Public stances and reports of what is happening are unhelpful.

- If talks fail, avoid shrill denunciations of the other negotiators: the calm acceptance of failure, in sorrow not anger, wins more votes in the public relations war. It also makes it easier for talks to recommence if, publicly, you are willing to have another go.
- Strike-bound employers should open the plants to employees who want to work if the strike is a substitute for negotiation.
- If you co-operate with the strikers in closing down your operation, you enhance the authority of the strike leaders over your employees. This is contrary to your INTERESTS.

"Subject to board approval"

You have been negotiating with the monkeys, not the organ grinders. There is always an organ grinder on the board who thinks he could do better than the monkeys, and he demonstrates his superiority by sending the AGREEMENT back with his amendments.

Counter: Pad offers that are subject to board approval.

Summarising

Simple but effective negotiating behaviour.

Negotiations are chaotic. The verbal interaction wanders. People join the flow of conversation and set it off at a tangent (or back to something already covered). Interruptions occur, both planned and unplanned. A summary refocuses attention on the issues:

- What has been said about them.
- What each side is proposing.
- What the differences are.
- What remains to be agreed.
- What has been agreed.

Summaries should be short (they are a summary not a blow-by-blow account) and neutral (cover each side's point of view and what they have proposed – unblemished by tone or grimaces).

A biased summary starts ARGUMENTS. A neutral summary placed in the middle of a long bout of verbiage, or when the debate wanders off into unhelpful territory, works wonders on even the most jaded or hot-tempered of negotiators.

Summarise during all phases of the negotiation, particularly:

- when argument dominates the exchanges;
- immediately after a PROPOSAL (then SHUT UP);
- when calling for agreement;

■ after agreement has been reached, to check that what you think you have agreed corresponds to what they believe.

Switch selling

A seller's ADD-ON tactic. You think you are negotiating to buy a deluxe model widget, but you find yourself being sold the super deluxe model. The seller has "switch sold" you up the range.

Sometimes this is to your benefit – the super deluxe is really more suited to your needs – but often it is not. They advertise a fantastic bargain. When you get there they have sold out of the "bargain" but they do have a few "slightly more expensive" versions available.

Counter: Insist it is the original deal or no deal.

Table

Like the VENUE, if it matters to one of you, it matters to both of you.

Negotiators like to sit behind a table, and not just to lay their papers or elbows on it. It is partly instinctive: a table "protects" you in the same way that you use your legs and arms to cover parts of your body when you feel threatened or unsure (see NON-VERBAL BEHAVIOUR).

Negotiations begin in conflict (your solution or mine) and end in co-operation (a jointly agreed solution). Putting something between you and them reassures your subconscious anxieties. If you did not feel comfortable you would perform less well, even display overt antagonism.

Some "experts", confusing cause for consequence, think you should force negotiators to sit next to each other in an "open" formation because they believe that tables exacerbate conflict.

The table in the Vietnam peace negotiations in the 1970s almost stopped the negotiations. Were there two parties, Vietnam and the United States, or four parties, North Vietnam, South Vietnam, the Vietcong and the United States?

In the Iraq–Iran peace negotiations neither party wanted to look at the other side. Eventually two tables were laid out in a "V" shape with the chairman at the top of the V and neither party looking at the other, only at the chairman.

Tables matter, as does the furniture, the caucus rooms and refreshments.

Tacit bargaining

Where communication is not possible, or extremely circumscribed, the parties make their moves on how they expect the other party to behave, or in reaction to how they perceive them to be behaving (see PRISONER'S DILEMMA).

In competition with a rival firm, you have a choice of increasing your PRICE or maintaining it (perhaps costs are rising and squeezing profits for both of you). As collusion between suppliers is illegal you face ruinous price competition, but through tacit bargaining based on past behaviour, you "agree" to raise prices, in the knowledge that your rival will follow your rise and not exploit your move by remaining at the lower price, so that you both restore your profits.

Take-off

Reverse the ADD-ON. A ploy to raise your PRICE safely, or when a buyer challenges your price and you have padded it.

You quote a price that covers your costs plus add-ons.

Seller: My normal price for this service is $700.
Buyer: That is far too high, and way outside our budget.

Take off a little.

Seller: You realise I have included my travel expenses in the price.
Buyer: A bit better but still …

Take off some more.

Seller: Plus my hotel expenses.
Buyer: I see.

You have entered the settlement range.
The take-off enables you to raise your price safely. If challenged

you retreat a little. If unchallenged, apply the add-on: add your expenses on top of the $700.

Target

The negotiating OBJECTIVE you aim to reach if you can. It is what you want to settle on.

If you open at your target you are likely to be forced to move away from it, unless they accept your FIRST OFFER.

Taxation

An avoidable but not evadable cost. If tax collectors believe that

- you owe them money in a clear-cut case,
- legal precedent and legislation are beyond doubt, and
- you can pay it,

they issue an instruction to pay and you pay up, subject to your right of appeal.

You can arrange payment terms with their consent, but you cannot demand them if you have:

- been caught evading payment;
- obstructed their investigations;
- prevaricated and used outright deceit.

You probably face a prison sentence too.

The tax collectors' interest is in collecting as much taxation as the law prescribes (personal promotion and their salaries depend on it). Thus where legal issues are complicated (nobody has yet devised an unambiguous tax system) and the outcome of an appeal to the courts is uncertain, the tax authorities are usually willing to negotiate how much you pay and when you pay it, in order to collect something for certain as opposed to an uncertain amount later, and to avoid the risk of losing the case and letting others know of the loophole you found (tax cases are widely publicised).

Teaching wolves to chase sledges

Offering futile CONCESSIONS to generate goodwill.

You are under pressure. The other negotiator is challenging you hard on PRICE. You think the best way to relieve the pressure is to concede something small. You do so. Nothing happens. The pressure continues so you concede something more with the same result. You are perplexed.

You ought not to be. Your behaviour is creating the pressure not relieving it. If you concede in the face of pressure, you teach other negotiators to pile on the pressure.

It is like trying to discourage wolves from chasing your sledge by throwing food to them. This does not work because you are teaching them that if they want to be fed, they should chase sledges.

(From a speech by a trade union militant at a meeting of striking tube train drivers in London, c1960s.)

Teamwork

Has advantages and disadvantages. Both can be optimised by PREPARATION and discipline.

The leader carries the bulk of the burden of conducting the negotiation and must make the tactical decisions and call the shots. People not directly involved can slip into the role of spectators, which, as any player will tell you, leads them to assume they can do better. They are tempted into interventions, not always well-timed and, in the extreme, they attempt *coups d'état* between meetings.

- Teams must be disciplined. The only appropriate time and place for criticism and dissent is during ADJOURNMENT, in a private caucus meeting and not in front of the other team.

- Who should be the leader? It is appropriate for the leader to be the best-qualified person, irrespective of seniority.

- What do the other members of the team contribute? If there is no obvious answer, why are they there? A lot of TIME is taken up with negotiation, and people who are not needed should do something more productive.

- Forming teams solely to match the other team's numbers is not sensible. A well-briefed team need not be the same size as the other side's. There is no "safety in numbers", only expense.

- Somebody SUMMARISING is a great help to the leader. Summaries provide well-needed breaks, reduce tension, refocus the negotiations on the issues and demonstrate that you and your team are LISTENING to what the other negotiators are saying.

- Experts and specialists can be consulted or invited to contribute on narrowly defined lines to the discussions. If technical issues are central to the negotiation, have people present who can contribute sensibly but ensure that they are commercially minded. Once technical people start drifting into technicalities they can destroy a commercial negotiating position. Interactions between your experts and those on the other side should be restricted (and kept within your sight and hearing).

- You often need an observer. It is always "easier" to analyse a negotiation from the observer's position than it is if you are contributing to what is going on. Adjournments give opportunities for the observer to contribute to the assessment of the state of play and to make recommendations for future actions.

■ Team should always prepare together. Unbriefed or partially briefed team members are dangerous allies. Someone "parachuting" into a negotiation who was not present during the preparation is lethal – people who negotiate together should prepare together.

Termination

Essential clause in any contract. A specified date for the termination of the current contract covers you against a perpetual contract that contains, because circumstances change, onerous consequences.

Termination for cause

Identifies the grounds on which a contract may be terminated for cause before the specified termination date. This appears in most commercial, and increasingly in personnel, contracts.

Grounds for termination for cause in commercial AGREEMENTS include:

■ a party entering into an arrangement with creditors;
■ the appointment of an administrator, receiver or liquidator;
■ ceasing, or threatening to cease, to trade;
■ being in breach of any material terms of the contract, including BREACH OF FIDUCIARY TRUST;
■ bringing the other party into disrepute or damaging its reputation;
■ non-performance of any obligation, including financial, not covered by FORCE MAJEURE.

Grounds for termination for cause in personnel agreements include:

- breach of trust, duty of care or fiduciary duty;
- accepting inducements or bribes from third parties;
- endangering the lives of employees or customers;
- acting in a racist, sexist, bullying or threatening manner;
- breaching safety and hygiene regulations or any laws applicable to the workplace;
- bringing the organisation into disrepute;
- leaking unauthorised statements to the media;
- conduct warranting dismissal under an organisation's disciplinary procedures, including instant suspension and dismissal for gross misconduct, and failure to improve performance after a final written warning.

In all termination with cause cases the issue of compensation from, or to, the parties may be subject to legal process, not a negotiation. To effect a termination, even with cause, and to obviate the high costs of a legal action, it is sometimes convenient to negotiate compensation and suppress public knowledge of the deal through a COMPROMISE AGREEMENT. Where commercial damage is caused, the parties may settle their differences in court. If termination is the result of bankruptcy, the damaged party may become a creditor.

Termination without cause

Identifies the grounds on which a contract may be terminated before the specified termination date. This clause is increasingly becoming a feature of commercial and personnel contracts, when the person involved fails to perform, when the termination compensation is attractive enough, or when the organisation wants to restructure.

Grounds for termination without cause in commercial agreements include:

- the agreement is not reaching, or is unlikely to reach, its financial targets and threatens to impose losses on a party;

- by mutual consent (sometimes a euphemism to save face);
- a party is taken over or relocated and is no longer in the business of the original agreement;
- a party intends to assign the original agreement.

Grounds for termination without cause in personnel agreements include:

- by mutual consent (almost always a euphemism for it's not working out);
- an employee gives notice of resignation;
- an employer wishes to reorganise or close down an activity (redundancy).

In all termination without cause cases, the main negotiating issue is whether compensation is due from, or to, a party. An employee resigning for any reason (unless by mutual consent) is not usually entitled to compensation but may be if it is part of a package on the grounds that the employee's resignation is convenient to the employer.

Boards that terminate the contract of a chairman, managing director, chief operating officer or financial director may be obliged under its terms to compensate the employee with the unexpired portion of the contract at its face value, or some multiple of it, and allow realisation of any share OPTIONS that would otherwise lapse. As these terms are unpopular with shareholders, it is best if such people insist that the board formally approves their personal terms before having to invoke them. Acrimonious parting brings out the worst in the parties, not their benevolence or compassion.

Thousand exceptions

A ploy to weaken the implementation of a policy.

Attacking a policy head-on is not always fruitful. The

momentum behind it is so great that it sweeps all before it. The thousand exceptions is a reverse SALAMI: instead of helping to introduce a policy by restricting its immediate application, you help undermine a policy by creating numerous exceptions.

Any policy is vulnerable when its practical details are considered. A general implementation could be limited by the sheer administrative cost of applying it everywhere at once.

- Discover awkward exceptions.
- Create exceptions.
- List exceptions.
- Don't indicate your total opposition to the theme of the policy (which its supporters would latch on to and isolate at once).

The more committed that you appear to be to the policy, the more convincing your "regret" that "unfortunately", for the moment, and with your current resources, it would be wiser to confine it to this limited application.

Threat

Unlike a promise, something that you prefer not to implement.

Threats are part of the repertoire of COERCION. There are two kinds:

- **Compliance.** Unless you do the following specific things, we will do the following to you.
- **Deterrence.** If you do the following things, we will do the following to you.

The consequences of a compliance threat can be avoided by doing what the threatener requires. Examples include threats to:

- go on STRIKE unless the company pays higher wages;
- attack unless a country withdraws its forces;

■ leave unless your partner stops drinking.

The consequences of a deterrent threat can be avoided by refraining from doing what the threatener objects to. Examples include threats to:

■ use force if you attack them;
■ go on strike if you sack employees;
■ leave if your partner starts drinking.

Threats are judged on:

■ the capability of the threateners to carry out the threat;
■ the likelihood of them doing so if thwarted in their other intentions;
■ their likely effects if they are implemented.

Threats raise the tension of a negotiation. A threat cycle is difficult to stop. People do not like to be threatened because, apart from the disagreeable consequences to them of the threats being implemented, they do not like to have their choices circumscribed. If they comply or desist, it appears they did so because of the threat, thus encouraging more threats, when they may, for other reasons, wish to adopt a course of action, or inaction, which corresponds to the threatener's preferences.

Threats may achieve their aims without being implemented, or they may not be believed and have to be implemented or withdrawn. A threat that achieves its ends without being implemented could be the result of a tactical adjustment by the other negotiators, who are temporarily unable under existing conditions to resist the threat. But as soon as those conditions change, they seek revenge.

■ Making specific threats is more convincing than being vague, but it is also more restrictive for the threatener. If the threat is ignored, the threatener has little choice but to implement the threat or lose credibility.

■ Private threats are more likely to succeed than public ones. If those threatened resent the public loss of face in succumbing to the threat, they might feel compelled to refuse to budge and force the threat to be implemented.

■ Vague threats leave the initiative to the threatener as to whether, or how, the threats are implemented, but the vaguer they are the less convincing they become.

■ Bluffing threats are risky because they might be called (loss of credibility). If you must BLUFF, be vague in your intentions, as this gives room for doubt about what triggers the threat's implementation. If those threatened suspect or believe (intelligence, own assessment of the situation) that you are bluffing, they could call your bluff and you could end up in a war or strike even though originally you were bluffing.

Time

The great pressuriser. Negotiations fill the time available, and if that is less than planned for, the negotiator moves faster or, more frequently, blows it.

Time pressure:

■ is uncomfortable;
■ adds stress to an already stressful situation;
■ forces hard choices;
■ can split a negotiating team apart, because team members' PERCEPTIONS of what is now possible do not change at the same rate.

Time can be compressed (we decide by 5pm) or extended (we will call you when we have considered all the PROPOSALS). In the former the negotiators are racing the clock; in the latter they are watching it.

Negotiators working against time prefer to postpone the other negotiators' making a decision until they have had the chance to influence that decision.

Negotiators kicking their heels waiting for a decision rapidly reach the point where they do not care what decision it is as long as it is a decision.

Counters

- Have more than one time plan for a negotiation (a long one and a short one), and be ready to work to whichever plan suits the time that becomes available.
- Maintain strong communication links between the negotiators and the home base, including regular briefing if possible.
- Adapt the negotiators to the time climate by sending in support if the negotiation is compressed (do not leave it to stressful meetings of pressurised team members), or by pulling out people if they can be used elsewhere while fully supporting those who are left.

Tit-for-tat

A win-win strategy. Robert Axelrod showed how the best STRAT-EGY for an indefinite run of dilemma plays is for the players to adopt tit-for-tat. A player co-operates on the first move and from then on does whatever the other player did on the previous move.

The strategy "teaches" the other players that the benefits of co-operation are available if they choose a co-operative OPTION (because you always respond positively), but that if they choose to defect, so will you. As the rewards to each from co-operation over the long run are greater than the rewards for defection (because defection is always punished), they have a strong incentive to co-operate.

Signalling co-operation without being exploited is the most difficult task facing a negotiator. Tit-for-tat is a workable strategy because it is obvious what you are up to and it is simpler than the alternatives.

It works best when the negotiators take a long-term view of the relationship. Short-term gains can overwhelm intentions to co-operate, even though the negotiators know this is irrational in the long run.

When playing tit-for-tat:

- never defect first;
- if the other negotiator defects react immediately, you have a low threshold to provocation;
- remember that a delayed response weakens your signalled message.

If they decide to co-operate again:

- forgive them instantly for their defection without rancour;
- immediately respond co-operatively;
- do not exact additional punishment "just to show them". Bring them to their senses, not to their knees.

Tough guy/nice guy

A ploy that works best on frightened negotiators. It is an act: two negotiators alternate between a tough, uncompromising, aggressive and COMPETITIVE STYLE, and a softer, more CO-OPERATIVE STYLE.

Naturally, you prefer to deal with the apparently softer person, but his "hands are tied" by his tougher colleague. He wants to help you but he needs you to help him. So you move closer to his position than you intended, but you are comforted by the illusion that this is a lot less far than you would have had to go to satisfy the "gorilla" who did all the shouting and made all those impossible demands.

You have been had. The duet was a set-up to make you concede. Neither is nicer nor nastier than the other. They compare notes afterwards and laugh all the way to the next negotiation.

Toughness

Much misunderstood as aggressive behaviour, instead of toughness in resolve. Tough negotiators:

- aim for the TARGET, having made proper PREPARATIONS beforehand;
- are not afraid of DEADLOCK and do not give up easily;
- open with a REALISTIC OFFER and move modestly;
- listen carefully to what the other negotiators say;
- closely scrutinise all the details of what the other party wants;
- only move conditionally (if you ... then I ...).

Toughness in resolve must not be confused with abrasive and aggressive manners. These are not necessarily an indication of resolve or intentions. Some extremely weak negotiating positions can be camouflaged by aggressive behaviour and are vulnerable to quiet, well-mannered responses, high in resolve, low on aggression.

Tradables

The currency of the BARGAINING process. They cover anything, tangible or intangible, over which either party has discretion. Movement is secured by offering to TRADE something that you have for something that they have.

Common tradables include the following.

- Money: PRICE, wages, finance, currency, credit, profits, income, taxes, bonds.
- TIME: when it happens, who to, who from, for how long.

- Goods: quantities, quality, features, substitutes.
- Specification: marginal changes, performance standards.
- Services: standards, personnel, performance.
- GUARANTEES: guarantor, liability, liquidated damages.
- WARRANTIES: duration, extent, coverage.
- RISK: extent, who carries it, shares.

As a negotiator, considering the tradables available to you gives you ideas for PREPARATION, new strategies, new PROPOSALS and new ways to get out of DEADLOCK.

Trade

Never give an inch: trade it. Trading constitutes the singular difference of negotiation compared with other forms of decision-making. What is traded may be:

- tangible or intangible;
- something in the present or a promise of something in the future;
- of value to both or only to one of the negotiators.

Trade involves exchange. One negotiator gives up something she has, or controls, or can promise for the future, in exchange for something the other negotiator has, controls or can promise.

Negotiation is about the terms of the trade: how much is given in exchange for how much is received.

Trade union

An employee's BARGAINING AGENT. In theory, most trade unions are run by their members; in practice, small minorities of "active" members run them. The quality of elections and decision-making processes varies widely. Some members are fiercely loyal to the union, but most blow hot and cold depending on circumstance. It rarely pays to make membership of the union an issue, unless it has gone over the top with serious misbehaviour (such as intimidation, political STRIKES).

Trust

Earned not deserved. Trust is unlikely to flourish when the negotiators are:

- suspicious of motives, intentions, capabilities or past behaviour;
- hostile for any reason;
- highly competitive;
- contesting vital issues;
- facing big gains or losses;
- feeling threatened;
- ignorant of each other;
- recent victims of trickery.

Trust flourishes when the negotiators have:

- demonstrated their reliability;
- experience of each other in a variety of circumstances;
- invested in confidence-building measures (see CONTINGENCY DEALS);
- reciprocated in helpful ways and not taken unfair advantage when they could have.

Does trust pay off? Not if its consequences are assumed without being tested. To trust anyone recklessly is as risky as dealing with someone who is totally untrustworthy.

If trust is earned by being of proven quality, it pays off handsomely. WIN-WIN outcomes are easier to arrive at if the negotiators are able to be open about their needs without fear of being exploited.

Mutual trust enables the negotiators to increase the size of the cake by exploring, in a safe atmosphere, new solutions to difficult problems.

Unconditional offer

Music to the ears of the other negotiators. An unconditional OFFER is a wasted offer. The other negotiators will accept the offer but come back for more. One-way conceding is no way to conduct a negotiation. Make conditional offers.

Used-car sale

A classic example of DISTRIBUTIVE BARGAINING. Neither you nor the seller knows the other's exit PRICE, or whether the first price mentioned is a SHAM OFFER or a TARGET price.

Treat a FIRST OFFER as an offer than can be improved upon. Whatever they open with, no matter how good it looks, HAGGLE. Convince sellers that:

- they prefer a sale on terms more favourable to you than they originally expected to get;
- your terms for the car are less favourable to them than they expect;
- a quick sale to you at a lower price than they want is better for them than waiting for another customer;
- you will settle at once if the price is right.

All your positive comments on the vehicle's characteristics, or the maker's reputation, or your need for it, undermine you stance.

Sellers ask early on what price range you are interested in. They are assessing your exit price, not saving you TIME looking through their range. So do not tell them. Ask to see their cars. Once sellers have invested time in trying to sell you a car, they are even keener to come to a deal.

- Take up their time.
- Ask QUESTIONS.
- Keep them waiting while you check every inch of the vehicle.
- Don't show keenness for a particular vehicle.
- Let them revise downwards their likely profit in order to close the deal.

Valuing concessions

It is not what it is worth to you that counts, but what it is worth to the other negotiator.

The temptation to give things away that are of little value to ourselves is universal. Value everything in the other negotiators' terms. Ask yourself: "What is it worth to them? If they want it, then they value it; and if they value it, what can I get back from them that I value?"

Negotiating is decision-making by trading. You TRADE things that are cheaper for you, but valued by the other negotiator, for things that are valued by you, but cheaper for the other negotiator.

Venue

Where negotiations take place is occasionally important to one or both negotiators. A home venue might be advantageous to one of the parties:

- They control the environment.
- They can manipulate the HOSPITALITY.
- They are closer to their coalition members whom they can consult.
- They have access to records, files, data.
- They are visibly "in charge" as hosts.

However, one party's advantage is not necessarily another party's disadvantage:

- They cannot walk out of their own premises.
- They cannot claim to have AUTHORITY, if the people with the alleged authority are nearby.
- Any failures in the services to the negotiation, or any embarrassments, are more likely to undermine the composure of the hosts than that of the guests.

When negotiating at the client's premises there is the problem of the security of your recess rooms and communications with your head office. If premature disclosure of your views on the situation is likely to undermine your position, you have fewer remedies on their home ground than you do on yours. (Make your call on your mobile in the car park; do not caucus in elevators.)

In dictatorships there are no neutral venues, and you can take it for granted that surveillance goes on irrespective of your status (they spy on each other, so what is so special about you?).

What are you looking for in an ideal venue?

- A good size negotiating room with space to walk about and work in comfort.
- Comfortable furniture, lighting and ventilation.
- Recess rooms for each team, with direct-dial and secure telephones, and access to the internet.
- Discreet venue staff who go about their work quietly and do not interfere in events.
- Everything cleaned and tidied during breaks, and all refreshments replenished regularly.

Vulnerability

Ask yourself where you are vulnerable in a business situation. It might help you to protect your flanks from surprises. For example:

■ A short-term lease leaves you vulnerable to a notice to quit when it's least convenient.

■ A long-term lease might bind you in when you see better opportunities elsewhere.

These considerations prompt you to cover your vulnerability in your PROPOSAL.

■ A management is vulnerable just before an order surge arrives. The employees might take advantage of the pressure to extract CONCESSIONS.

■ An absent partner is vulnerable to decisions made without him or her.

■ A supplier is vulnerable to competition offering similar lines.

■ We are all vulnerable to accidents.

Thinking about vulnerabilities is productive if it produces constructive measures to avert being ambushed when least expected or welcomed.

Waking up the dead

A risky intervention ploy. Faced with determined negotiators and not making much progress, it is tempting to try to explore differences of view in their team. You invite a member of the other team who has remained silent throughout the session to comment.

- "What do you think, Mr Sujamo?"
- "Have you any suggestions about how to break this impasse, Ms Allbright?"

You are taking a RISK. The other negotiators might resent your interference and retaliate by stiffening their position. If the team is disciplined, you are unlikely to succeed.

Walk-out

It does not always work. They do not come running after you; they leave you to stew.

- Are you walking out to signal your disapproval of something they have said, suggested, done or implied?
- Can you demonstrate disapproval in some other way?
- Why not tell them what you feel?
- What do you do when you are faced with a walk-out by the other negotiators?

As a pressure ploy it lacks a focus, because it is not clear what the other negotiators are meant to do when you walk out. The other team might believe that you are serious about your stance and accommodate you, but they might also regard you as unstable.

If it is a COLLECTIVE BARGAINING dispute, a diplomatic problem, or a spouse argument, walking out might bring things to a head, though not necessarily in the way you intended (they wanted you to go on STRIKE, to DEADLOCK, to abandon the matrimonial home, and so on, so they provoked you to walk out).

How do you recommence negotiations after a walk-out unless you specify when you will be back? Why not lower the temperature or significance of the walk-out by calling for an ADJOURNMENT, even an abrupt one to "cool off", to "think about things", to seek advice, and so on. It is much easier to resume negotiations after an adjournment than after a walk-out. There is no embarrassment or social awkwardness when you return at the specified time or date you announced when you adjourned.

Warranty

Present in most AGREEMENTS (see also CONTRACT LAW). Ignore warranties at your peril because breach of your warranties (you do not perform as promised, your "facts" were not true, you had no power to contract, you had already sold it to someone else, you do not own what you sold, you lied about your business accounts, and so on) can terminate the agreement and allow the other party to claim damages.

Warranty clauses require your close attention. Warranties are time bombs awaiting an opportunity to go off. When they do, they cost a great deal, and courts will uphold them because they regard your warranties as the GUARANTEE of your honesty. If events prove otherwise, your reputation and your net worth are at risk of the court's severest displeasure. Never sign a warranty that you know, or suspect, to be less than 100% true.

Careful negotiators require you to provide warranties for all your claims and promises, and if necessary will enforce your warranty by its close cousin, known as an INDEMNITY.

"We should have been told"

A disavowal of responsibility ploy.

You have exceeded an agreed budget and want an additional payment for the extra work you have undertaken. They deny responsibility because "they should have been told" before you incurred extra expenses. As you did not tell them, they refuse to pay, no matter that the additional work was necessary. You are stuck with the cost.

Try to negotiate an official variation order system under which all variations to the contract must be authorised by a named official if payment is to be made, and in return, if an official variation order is made, the client guarantees payment of the extra costs.

Counter: Always tell them when extra work is required and do nothing until they agree. If the roof collapses before they agree, tell them that "you should have been told" that you had a blank cheque to do whatever was necessary.

"What do you know?"

A long-shot ploy to elicit information.

The other negotiators open by asking you how much you know about the issues. You tell them. They find out more about your knowledge of the details than perhaps you intended to let them know at this stage. Your selection and presentation of detail also signal your PRIORITIES.

Counter: "Not a lot. Perhaps you could go over the issues for me."

What if?

QUESTIONS to elucidate potential negotiable issues. Useful when faced with DEADLOCK. It helps to explore possible solutions to the deadlock.

Q: What if we were to consider delaying the payment deadlines, would that help you with your budgeting?

Also useful when faced with a proposition that may look all right but you have no criteria against which to judge it.

Q: What if you make $200,000 instead of $50,000 in the first year? What larger share would I get in those circumstances?

A checklist of "what if" questions drawn up before you negotiate is a useful PREPARATION tool.

Win-win

I win, you win, so we both win. The goal of an effective negotiator (see NON-ZERO SUM).

In negotiating there are four possible outcomes defined in terms of winning or losing:

1 We both win.
2 I win, you lose.
3 I lose, you win.
4 We both lose.

We both lose in a DEADLOCK. The TIME spent negotiating could have been used for something more profitable, and we may experience long-term disagreeable consequences (such as litigation).

Either of us winning with the other losing is likewise an unattractive outcome. If I win at your expense (I sell you a failing business as a going concern), I risk destroying my reputation or our relationship. If for any reason you are unhappy with the deal, or how we arrived at it, my winning is a Pyrrhic victory. It could cost me dear later (see INDEMNITY).

The win-win outcome is the most desirable. It gives both of us a stake in the implementation of the AGREEMENT. On the basis of our experience, both of us are willing to consider doing more business in future and to pass on our helpful judgments about each other to third parties.

Winner's curse

Often experienced by negotiators when a FIRST OFFER is accepted, or the other side accepts any OFFER too quickly. It leaves you with the feeling that your offer was pitched too low/too high and that you missed an opportunity to do better out of the deal.

Counters: Proper PREPARATION of your entry terms and careful phrasing of your tentative PROPOSALS.

Yes, but

A closing ploy.

"Your offer is acceptable, but for one small point." You meet the point in some way, and then expect agreement. "Fine," they reply. "But there is this other detail we must settle." If you settle that issue too, another one will pop up, and for as many acceptances as you make, in a desperate bid to reach agreement, they produce another "yes, but".

Counters

- At the first "yes, but", ask for any other problems they may have, and consider them together in a package.
- Retaliate with "no, but": "I cannot accept movement on this small detail, but if you were to move on this other point, I am prepared to consider a change in what you are now seeking." This puts a PRICE on their "yes, buts" and they know that you will price any changes they care to introduce.

Yesable proposition

A seller's ploy based on the momentum generated by buyers saying yes to a series of questions. If they keep saying yes, they will eventually say yes to the closing proposition to buy the product (in theory).

Q: Do you have a problem with copying costs?
A: Yes.
Q: You accept that the Corex Copier copies more times per cent than any other copier on the market?

A: Yes.

Q: You want to start making big savings on copier costs right away?

A: Yes.

Q: Will you okay this request for a Corex Copier for delivery in 72 hours?

A: Yes.

It's not always so obvious, but it is likely to be tried on you from time to time.

"You win some and you lose some"

Do not underestimate the need to save face; it motivates almost everybody. You have put a lot of effort into an issue, argued long and strong for an outcome, perhaps thrown in the odd THREAT or two, but in the end you realise you cannot get anything like what you want.

What do you do? Press on with the conflict? It is often better from the negotiator's point of view to admit defeat gracefully. Make light of your loss:

▪ Well, George, you win some and you lose some, and this is not my winning day.
▪ That's life. It was worth a try.

Zz

Zero sum

Jargon from GAME THEORY: what you gain, they lose.

Your INTERESTS are diametrically opposed; you are in a state of pure conflict.

Some (difficult) negotiations and HAGGLES are zero-sum games (see NON-ZERO SUM). In pure conflict negotiations you perceive your opponent to be trying to gain at your direct expense. There can be no co-operation or collusion between you to find a mutually advantageous solution because all solutions (except you winning) are mutually disadvantageous.

Zeuthen's conflict avoidance model

Compares the gains likely to be made by accepting what is on offer with the NET gains likely to be made by conflict (a STRIKE or a LOCK-OUT).

- There is a range of practicable bargains (the settlement range), and any wage rate within this range is more advantageous to either party than a conflict.
- Outside the settlement range ("the fighting sphere"), compromise is less advantageous than resort to conflict.
- The limits to fighting are given by the expected result of fighting plus or minus the expected fighting costs.
- The workers will not accept a wage rate lower than they could receive by a fight minus the losses they take by going on strike.
- The employers will not pay a wage higher than they could be

forced to by a fight plus the losses they take by contesting a strike.

Zeuthen's model is a two-stage process. The bargainers compare the certain value obtainable from accepting the other party's current OFFER with the expected value they obtain by holding to their current demands together with the expected value of a breakdown in the negotiations and mutual resort to conflict. This calculation produces the maximum probability of conflict they are willing to accept in preference to accepting the other side's current offer.

The bargainer whose willingness to accept the RISK of conflict is smallest (the one who is most anxious to avoid conflict) is the one who makes the next CONCESSION. If it is the worker's AGENT, the union demand for a wage increase is reduced; if it is the employer, the company's wage offer is increased.

The size of a bargainer's concession is determined by how much a particular concession increases their willingness to risk a strike if it is unacceptable to the other side. Naturally, each party endeavours to persuade the other that any move short of the gap between them induces a preference for a strike (raising their apparent "eagerness for a fight" in the PERCEPTION of their opponent).

Mistaken assessments of the other's eagerness for a fight, or miscalculations of your own net benefits of conflict, lead to a negotiated wage rate above or below what was practicable if the parties had made different assessments. It boils down to an assessment of which of the parties feels strong enough to resort to, or ride out, conflict.

Appendices

1 Negotiation training resources

25 Role Plays to Teach Negotiation
Asherman, I.G. and Asherman, S.V. (Vol. 2, HRD Press, 2003)

The Negotiation Sourcebook
Asherman, I.G. and Asherman, S.V. (2nd edition, HRD Press, 2003)

Fifty Plus Activities to Teach Negotiation
Asherman, I.G. (HRD Press, 1996)

All available in the UK from:
Management Learning Resources
PO Box 28
Carmarthen
Dyfed SA31 1DT
Tel: +44 1267 281 661

And in the United States from:
HRD Press
22 Amherst Road
Amherst, MA, 01002-9709
Website: www.hrdpress.com

Kennedy's Simulations for Negotiation Training
Kennedy, G. and Kennedy, F. (3rd edition, 2007)
Available from:
Ashgate Training
Gower House
Croft Road
Aldershot
Hants GU11 3HR, UK
Website: www.gowertraining.co.uk

Online resource

Negotiation Workshop
Pre-course materials, exercises, simulations, cases

Available from:
Negotiate Ltd
Website: www.negotiate.co.uk

University accredited distance-learning courses

Negotiation (1992; 2nd edition, 2000)
Influence (2001)
Strategic Negotiation (2006)
Elective MBA and MSc courses, combining printed textbooks, full online support packages, including faculty boards, FAQs, recent past examination papers and solutions. Accredited by Heriot-Watt University (Edinburgh Business School); twice-yearly examinations for University Certificates at over 350 centres worldwide.

Published by:
Edinburgh Business School
Heriot-Watt University
Riccarton
Edinburgh EH14 4AS, UK
Website: www.hw.ac.uk/home/dir/49/edinburgh-business-school

Video package

Do We Have a Deal?
25 minutes, includes trainer's guide, participant's notebook

Available from:
Ashgate Training (see above)

2 Specialised consultancies and trainers

CAPITA (formerly the Industrial Society)
Website: www.info@capita-ld.co.uk
Industrial relations negotiation

Chartered Institute of Personnel Development
Website: www.cipd.co.uk
Full range of professional courses for HR

Coverdale Organisation
Website: www.coverdale.com
General negotiation training

Simon Gardner
Lanser, Luchana 2
48008 Bilbao, Spain
E-mail: sgardner@lanser.es
Negotiation courses in English and Spanish

Patrick Harlington
E-mail: patrick@ansabd.co.uk
Negotiation and sales courses

Huthwaite International
Website: www.huthwaite.co.uk
Sales and negotiation courses

Rudi Ionescu
Resources, Development and Ideas
E-mail: RDI@pcnet.ro
Negotiation and mediation consultancy

Interlink Partners
E-mail: linkpartners@compuserve.com

Sales and negotiation courses

Karrass Europe
Website: www.Karrass.co.uk and www.Karrass.com
The world's largest negotiation training company

Florence Kennedy
Negotiate Ltd
E-mail: florence@negweb.com
Website: www.negotiate.co.uk
Negotiation consultancy and training

Jack Quinlan and Associates
Website: www.negotiation.co.za

Colin Rose
E-mail: rose@netcon.net.au
Negotiation consultancy and training

3 Recommended reading

Abramowitz, A.J., *Architect's Essentials of Contract Negotiation*, John Wiley, New York, 2002.

Craver, C.B., *Legal Negotiation and Settlement*, 4th edition, Matthew Bender & Co., New York, 2001.

Craver, C., *The Intelligent Negotiator: What to Say, What to Do, How to Get What You Want – Every Time*, Prima Lifestyles, 2002.

Fisher, R. and Ury, W., *Getting to Yes: Negotiating Agreement Without Giving In*, 2nd edition, Penguin, New York, 1992.

Kennedy, G., *Everything is Negotiable*, 4th edition, Random House, London, 2008.

Kennedy, G., *The New Negotiation Edge: A Behavioural Approach for Results and Relationships*, Nicholas Brealey, London, 1998.

Kennedy, G., *Strategic Negotiation*, Gower, Aldershot, 2008.

Lewicki, R. et al., *Negotiation Readings, Exercises, and Cases*, 5th edition, McGraw-Hill, Chicago, 2006.

Lewicki, R.J. and Hiam, A., *Mastering Business Negotiation : A Working Guide to Making Deals and Resolving Conflict*, Jossey-Bass, San Francisco, 2006.

Litvak, M., *Dealmaking in the Film and Television Industry from Negotiation through Final Contracts*, 2nd edition, Silman Jones Press, Los Angeles, 2002.

Mnookin, R., Pepet, S.R. and Tulemello, A.S., *Beyond Winning: Negotiation to Create Value in Deals and Disputes*, Harvard Bellknap, Cambridge, 2000.

Raiffa, H., *The Art and Science of Negotiation*, Harvard University Press, Cambridge, 2005.

Shell, G.R., *Bargaining for Advantage: Negotiating Strategies for Reasonable People*, 2nd edition, Penguin, New York, 2006.